biologically
based

biologically based

A series of personal essays about the Body[1]
by Omni Kitts Ferrara

Dedication:

Daryl,
I offer this work to you, with great respect for us. I love
you through it all, as long as our cells may carry us.

Isla, Willa & Lil,
May this book hold a piece of the vast wisdom that is
your lineage, so that you feel empowered in who you
are. You are the beauty of what Life can be and I love
you so much.

"You your best thing"

-Toni Morrison[1]

Table of Contents

Foreword:

Everyone has a body. Everyone has a story and...

Every story is written in the Body. Omni Kitts Ferrara was my teacher and mentor first and then one day at her Yoga studio, she said to me, "I want to be your friend. We need to hang out and talk."

Reflecting back on that moment, I realize that it had already happened, we were already friends, deep and intimate. Our Bodies had been telling each other our respective stories through hours of practice, teacher training (I completed both my 200-hour and 500-hour with Omni), retreats, hikes, philosophical lectures, workshops, and community gatherings. It happened naturally and over time. Omni balks at the use of the word guru and has been known to announce quite vehemently that, "I have no desire to be a guru, that is not what we do

here. If you want that, you have the wrong studio."
Is Omni a guru? Omni is an expert in her field,
which is so much more than the American
conventional definition of a Yoga teacher, or an
occulted figure driven by narcissism that feeds off
of the natural human instinct to find meaning. She
is a master mover, an advanced experiential learner,
and mediator between the mind, Body, and pain.
Her teaching is driven by philosophy that puts the
focus on the student, that emBodies difference, that
allows for it all, and that does not answer the
questions for the student, but simply asks good
questions upon good questions. She holds space
and is a carrier of information passed down from
teacher to teacher to teacher and from Mother to
Mother to Mother. She brings the student, long
disconnected from their own Body, back to
conscious relationship with their Body. This
approach was a turning point for me personally
after years of Yoga and other physical practice,

unprocessed trauma, addiction, and recovery. In fact, I turned to this community as part of recovery. And now in this series of personal essays, Omni offers experiential evidence generously shared from her own Life and study. She exemplifies and models the power of this conscious relationship to heal, to engage with the world fully, and to expand and understand our own individual expression of pain -- to move through and listen to the wisdom of the Body. She says to pain, "I want to be your friend. We need to hang out and talk."

She knows full well that it has already happened; that we are always in relationship. Pain is already a friend, deep and intimate. We are all *biologically based*. The mind is PART of the Body, not apart from the Body. The Self, spirit, soul, whatever one names that seemingly separate part of consciousness, is PART of the Body, held by the Body. The story of each individual and the story of

Us is told chapter by chapter, through the backstory of ancestors, and with epilogues yet to be written. One of the most powerful aspects of this book is that it is a living document, in the throws of continuous editing. And as the editor, I know that this means work, a lot of work. This is good work, work that has worth, work that is, dare I name it, sacred. The stories and information here are applicable to anyone that lives in a Body regardless of the specific experience in that Body. Trust and believe the story of others. Trust and believe your own story. Trust and believe the Body.

Alison C. Solomon

Introduction:

Aren't introductions strange? I am supposed to tell you about why I am valuable and why my words are worth reading. Or give you insight into my magnificence. Well, let's be clear.

I am basically a nobody as far as western standards go. I am writing about the Body, but I am not a doctor. I am writing, but I am also not an author. That title assumes the understanding and expertise of language. At best, I am a wannabe writer. I feel it is vital to lower your expectations immediately. I will also not guarantee a logically linear thread to this book -- that nonsense is for the patriarchy. Expect an exercise in receptivity. You may feel lost as you read this book, seeking "the point." Here is where I will remind you that there is no set point. You will receive something, and many points may lead you back to more questions; none of which I have answers for. That is your space. That is your beautiful work.

Confusion doesn't have to be an enemy. Perhaps you will be annoyed and pissed off enough that you forge a new path somewhere else. I hope this book is evocative and jostles you for connection. I hope that as you read, you take it all personally, that you relate to your journey. You might rethink your experience and open up doors you have not allowed before.

If you only read material from MDs and PHDs and discount everything else -- well, that is called value attribution bias, look it up. Bias is a cognitive error. However, you are free and invited to do as you wish, so if you need a stamp of approval from academia as validation to read a book, then *put. the book. down.*

Hi, I'm Omni.

I was born to two professional dancers and have been watching movement since I was very little. My parents are performers, and some of my earliest memories include my living room filled with balloons and flower bouquets for my parents' singing telegram business. They danced, taught, and hustled. My Father is an incredible athlete/ dancer/ singer/ actor. My Mother is a choreographer /Julliard dancer /teacher/ director extraordinaire. I grew up living la vie Boheme.

Movement and art embedded in everything and are essential to my story.

"One of the grand strategies nature uses to construct nervous systems is to overproduce neural elements, such as neurons, axons and synapses, and then prune the excess."[1] Which means that we are all born with the possibility of more connections than we will ever need. Interestingly, the synapses are formed through our relationship to the outside world. Moving and interacting with our external environment curates the connections we make. This is why talking, holding and caring for young babies is so very important. Every touch, every sound informs the growing connections in the brain. Furthermore, where and how we grow up influences not only the synapses made but the ones kept as well. During certain phases of brain development, the Body prunes lesser used synapses to strengthen ones used most often. In essence, like snowflakes, each brain is unique. We are what we do the most. Like a bookmark on your favorites tab, the circuits used most are grooved, remembered, and prioritized.

My brain saw movement on an everyday basis. Movement grooved my brain and informed my being. I viscerally remember my Father's rehearsals, watching as he lifted other dancers over his head, making it look effortless, or standing alongside my Mother as she taught afternoon dance classes to young children. Repeatedly watching dance and movement created a synaptic network in me, a bodily knowing of non-verbal communication and action.

I have more time in my field of expertise than most at my age. Like Neo in the Matrix, I don't see things in 1s and 0s -- I see in Body actions of dorsiflexion and hip extension, motor control, and propulsion. I see Bodies in muscle, bones, and connective tissue. I study the activity of the nervous system. I break down movement into bodily sensations in profound ways. I work to articulate that complexity and encourage others to know their own complexity.

Movement is my Life.

I watched movement for a long time before I joined in. My Mother often said I was an observant child, watching first, and participating when I felt safe. I started dancing at 14, which is late as the dance world goes. I began helping my parents out with their summer dance residencies. I did some minimal recreational dance classes and then started taking a bus by myself to NYC at 15. I was lucky enough to participate in a summer intensive at the American Dance Festival in North Carolina. That summer inspired me to pursue dance in college. I auditioned and applied for scholarships and attended a state university in 1998. Two Dance conservatory programs later, I completed my BFA in Dance. After college, in search of an exercise modality, I started taking Yoga. I then found work at a Yoga studio.

I began to study anatomy and the Body. I learned new ideas and concepts every day from my boss/teacher, Vishali Varga.[2] In Yoga Teacher Training, I was introduced to Eastern philosophies, specifically Indian thought and the lexicon of spirituality. I also began to work and teach within a community who shared their stories with me: their losses, successes, health, illness, disease, trauma, injuries, and everything in between. I learned along with them.

Today, I am lucky enough to own this same Yoga studio.[3] I have clocked 18 years with this same community, 33,000+ teaching hours, 6000+ formal training hours, and endless off-the-books learning hours. I am a modern-day pattern keeper, a maestra, and a data collector.

I will offer some takeaways on movement intertwined with my personal experience and how my journey of Self-study empowered and affirmed my Life. Learning through my Life experience has been essential to my survival.

We all must learn to claim our experience -- that is a big part of why I wrote this book in the first place. I am a woman. I am a woman who has endured trauma. At 17, I was raped and kept it to myself because I thought it was my fault and didn't want to burden my family. The timing of this rape stunned my young emerging Self. In a moment, I was interrupted. My excitement to conquer the world quickly redirected to fierce protection from the world. One way I dealt with the trauma was an eating disorder, which eventually landed me in an in-patient recovery program.

I am a Mother of three girls who teach me the most about the Body. I have lived with postpartum and cultivate my mental health daily. I have investigated and advocated for my family's health from my knowledge of the Body. I am resilient because I have endured. I am still growing up and finding trust in my capacity.

I speak from the truth of who I am so that you might embrace your fullness too. Let's begin.

Take a comfortable seat.

Make sure you have support around you so that your Body can relax into the structures beneath and beside you.
I want to write to you in such a way that you can hear it.

And feel safe.

I want to write to you, so you feel included and valuable. If you are alive, you are already a success.

So let's just wait here.

Let us P A U S E.

Come close.

Move in.

Huddle near.

Land here.

Feel its welcome.

Let your cells relax.

Invite your breath to expand.

Blink your eyes slowly as if each blink was a snapshot of a particular moment for your brain to tag and store for later days.

Follow this space.

Follow the feeling within your being.

Feel your physical sensations.

What do you notice?

1: Learning through the lens of the Body.

It is all happening.
What we know
What we don't know
What we feel but cannot speak.
What we could not even imagine imagining
It is all real.
Our worst nightmares
Our best dreams.

We forget that no one knows why we are here.
Everyone fills the _____.
We are allowed to fill it.
We are allowed to disagree
Choice is not the common narrative, but it is our
nature.
What you choose can put you in danger
Freedom is not created by the government, it is
who you are.
The vastness contained by only what we can
perceive.
By what we were taught
By what we experienced
By what we see
By what we learn
By what we choose

Everything is allowed.
All of it.

It is here, materialized, embodied
Empowered by its being, inherently
Matter has weight
You are matter.
You have weight in the world
You pull and push the world
As the world presses on you concurrently.

You can make all the "right" choices and still lose;
You can do everything "wrong" and still win.

May you settle into your Life.
In your skin.
In the momentum
With resignation and resolve.

May you find wonder and curiosity in how you
respond and engage the world.
May you be surprised by your own choices
Because they are just choices.
All with consequence.
You are the consequence of others' choices.
You come from something.

It's all happening.
Everything is allowed.

• • •

At age 12, my Father gave me the book *Illusions* by
Richard Bach, a story about a reluctant Messiah
who quits and becomes a mechanic. It was such an
essential book to me that my first two tattoos pay
direct homage to the story[1], a blue feather, and a
red bi-plane. Many other narratives followed:
Siddhartha and *Demian* by Hermann Hesse, *King
Lear*, *The Diary of Anne Frank*.

I felt akin to these characters. Like they were trying
to give me a clue about the secret of the Multiverse.
They were asking the same questions that lived
inside of me, that came up every day.

Why am I here?
What is the point of all of this?
What am I supposed to be doing?

This line of questioning started way before I was
12, and was coupled with bodily sensation. For as

far back as I can remember, I remember f e e l i n g
things and then wondering, what does that mean?
Hunger, irritation, a paper cut, the wind, arousal,
sleepiness, what does that mean? I have identified
with my visceral sense of Self for my entire Life.
Visceral: the way you know something as expressed
through physical sensation or emotion in your
Body. For instance, when you feel it in your bones
or get goosebumps listening to someone sing. You
know something through feeling *first*, then
cognition.

As a young child, I connected with these physical
sensations to know the world. I trusted them. I can
recall staring at a blade of grass feeling the physical
sense of admiration and wonder in my skin. These
physical sensations were so yoked to my learning
the world that I can still conjure up their sense
memory. I can again feel my head on my Mother's
chest and the way I could settle in between her
breasts. Or the perfectly rounded edges of my
Grandmother's nails, a project she curated on an
everyday basis. The juxtaposition of the smooth
edges and the tensile strength always intrigued me.
My memories formed through feeling and then
accessed by cognition and question.

I also loved to think about my Body and its many feelings. Many nights I would lie in bed and stretch one arm up to the sky. I would stack the bones of my arms perpendicular to the bed until it felt effortless to hold up my arm. I would play this brainy game of aligning the bones of my arms so that they felt weightless, conduits for gravity, no longer held in tension. It was so relaxing it would often lull me to sleep. A paradoxical lullaby of sorts -- efficient bone stacking that led to full-Body relaxation.

It was also difficult to feel so much. Having an acute awareness of my Body was overwhelming at times. No other 8 year old I knew expressed any similar experience. My next-door neighbor was not starting girl-talk like, "Isn't it weird when someone enters the room, and you can feel that they are angry?" I could have written an essay on the physiological effects of my Body, from head to toe, after watching the musical *Grease*. This 8 year old iteration of myself was also afraid of everything: thunderstorms, ball pits, bees -- a worrywart from way back with actual warts to prove it. Ball pits seem like a colorful sea of fun, right? As a young kid, I had convinced myself that there was no floor beneath the balls. I thought the balls gave way to the center of the Earth, a slip and slide of sorts right into the Earth's core of molten Lava. Maybe it was the influence of all those 1980s movies and scenes of quicksand. The protagonists of *Indian Jones*, *Star Wars*, and *The Neverending Story* all faced that unforgiving ground. I think I inferred the same danger onto the ball pits. I can remember a period of time where it seemed like every birthday party was at McDonald's, a two hour session of hamburgers and the indoor play place. There was always a ball pit. I was a heavier child and endured enough bullying as it was, so I was not about to draw more attention to myself for being afraid of ball pits. So, I would will myself into the balls and pretend like I was having fun while bicycling my legs furiously to keep my Body up. It was exhausting. I was so relieved when it was time to eat hamburgers.

Nothing was wrong with me, but at times I felt like the noise in my Body was too much. There was this seemingly wide gap between what I was experiencing and what everyone else was experiencing. Or at least that is what it seemed like. I had already learned that emotion and sensation were not preferred topics of everyday living. I learned this understanding through every "shhh" and "stop-it." It became clear that when I was more emotional or wild, that was not preferred, especially out in public spaces. I could feel this unspoken rule that stated, "You just don't talk about emotions everywhere." I did not understand the reasoning behind this rule, but I knew I had less conflict if I just followed it. When I was emotional, I felt my parents' uncomfortability with that expression, so I kept it to myself, mostly. Now as a parent myself, I get it.

Even as I wondered about my complexity, I loved myself. I trusted my Body. I had a relationship with the unwavering aspect of my being. You might call it a soul; I call it my nervous system. I genuinely do not know what it is, I just know that eternality is there. We all get to fill that space however we wish. I know it now, and I knew it then because this eternal energy felt like something -- an ongoing "Rudy chant" in me. Yes, you can! You can do it! Get up! I've got your back!

Did you know that we all start as one single commingled cell of two sets of DNA information? This zygote then replicates and differentiates, on its own volition, eventually[2] becoming ~37.2 trillion cells. Our entire being emanates from one single cell. Furthermore, these cells are self-assembling and organizing for no apparent reason beyond living. We are complex Life forms here from our ancestors of bacteria, archaea, and protists.[3] And just like them, WE WANT TO LIVE. We all want to live. Our Bodies fight for Life as long as they can, so even as an 8 year old, I could consciously identify that drive to Live within me.

We are biologically based beings, all fighting for Life and food, living in a cultured world that we made up. Culture begins with the same questions I started this chapter with:

Why am I here?
What is the point of all of this?
What am I supposed to be doing?

In turn, homosapiens made shit up. It is hard to rest in uncertainty and the vastness of the Universe; "Evidence strongly suggests that humans in all cultures come to cast their own identity in some sort of narrative form. We are inveterate storytellers."[4] Narrative has served as a form of trying to know our existence to know our location in the infinite. The part that becomes problematic is that everyone thinks that their story is the *right* one. Dominance and violence ensue in an endless cycle of displacement and biased cooperation.

Let us not forget, we are a bunch of self-assembling bubbles. Chill.

Story has helped us survive and also continues to be the death of us. Religion, morality, and narrative are all things we choose to believe and repeat. No one knows what the heck is happening here. That confusion is our shared experience.

I was lucky enough to grow up without a religious paradigm forced upon me. Thank you, Mom and Dad. I appreciated their take on the Universe and was offered some great food for thought, but I was allowed to decide how I wanted to organize the cosmos. Even by them acknowledging the space to choose, they affirmed that there is no single universal answer for everything. The space they provided allowed room for both the ideas of Gods/Goddesses and evolutionary biology to be present. They didn't have to be mutually exclusive.

I grew up in the 1980s, rocking a mean side pony. The cultural programming of that era was strong. The *me generation*[5] looked through the lens of everything always works out, popularity gets the guy/girl and greed is good. In hindsight, it is a cesspool of white supremacy, sexism, hetero-normative ideals, and consumer culture.

My nature and cultured upbringing started to converge into this very palpable sense of confusion: all these feelings, no answers, and no religion to assuage any of it. I was 12, seeking and searching for the answers to the Universe, hoping that I could be Richard in the book *Illusions* and find my own Donald Shimoda, who would help me find my messiah status. It is interesting to see how the subliminal narcissism of the 1980s rhetoric was so strong that I was hoping to be the messiah. Now, this makes my stomach turn.

Ultimately, the answers I found left me uncontented. I often landed on the "Universe has a plan." I knew I had a place in the world. I knew I had some agency in the world, but something didn't fit. I needed more perspective. I was seeking a more complex answer that felt like my experience, versus how my experience was cultured. Then attending College, as a dance major, presented even more to consider.

I had never had the undying urge to just dance! I came to it later. I watched my parents dance my whole Life and developed quite an eye for it. As a teen, I could critique modern Dance better than most NYC critics. Initially, Dance was a place to make my Body do what other people wanted my Body to do. I liked the positive feedback of success. Dance changed my Body. As a semi-heavy child/teen losing weight from Dance invited a new form of attention. The vain acceptance of my high school peers felt nice, but simultaneously discounted my value in a bigger Body. It still left me feeling undervalued.

In college, Dance expanded, and I started to experience the art my parents always had felt in their hearts. I remember my favorite class with Nancy Bannon[6] it started with Laban/Bartenieff[7] articulations through the Body's joints and ended with a dynamic movement sequence across the floor, Body sensation in full force. Simultaneously, I was also wrestling with my inner waves, trying to control what felt genuinely unruly -- so I curbed eating. Too much. This landed me in an in-patient eating disorder facility early in my Sophomore year of college. This period marks the most challenging behavior toward my Body. My eating disorder was a cultured control mechanism aimed at not feeling what I was feeling. It was an avoidance technique.

My dance career had a lot of destructive tendencies tied to it. In one solo performed my senior year in college, I'm pretty sure I fractured my spine trying to achieve a grotesque looking backbend for the aesthetic of the piece. Needless to say, when I came to Yoga in my early twenties and asked the teacher, you mean, it isn't normal to have back pain every moment of every day? I was shocked to hear her response, "No, not at all."

At 21, just after I graduated from college, I was introduced to Yoga. I wasn't looking for a spiritual awakening, rather, I was looking for exercise. During my very first class, I was immediately intrigued. I was unimpressed with the plan the Universe had for me thus far. The Judeo-Christian model never resonated with me either. I needed a structure to consider myself. I was flailing about, looking for something to ground me in my experience. Life was becoming more uncomfortable. The sensations of my Body now included suppressed rape, PTSD, pain from overuse in Dance, eating disorder behaviors, and your run-of-the-mill trying to figure out Life feelings.

The same identification with my Body did not go away, it intensified.

I began to work at the Yoga studio.[8] Every day I had the privilege of learning Yoga plus greeting people, folding blankets and sweeping. I took class almost every day, and soon enough embarked on Teacher Training. Yoga expanded my horizon by sharing the history and philosophies of India. It is here that I learned structures to help me leverage the world. It offered me processes that worked to help me feel anchored in my Life. Now, as a teacher, I am so grateful to share these same concepts.

At the Yoga studio, we would host philosophy lectures, as well as asana workshops. In one lecture, a renowned scholar, Professor Douglas Brooks,[9] spoke on the concept of karma. Karma was a term I had heard while growing up. The way that I had understood it was, what goes around comes around. It felt full of doom and morality. It was a scary term with a threat embedded in it -- do good things or else. Furthermore, if I mess up, that mistake will get me. I was almost nervous to hear him talk about it.

And then he said, "The world is not conspiring FOR you or AGAINST you. The Universe is a power-based Universe, not a moral one."

He continued to explain a, new for me lens, of the Universe. One that did not stem from the Judeo-Christian model of a moral Universe. He described a Universe of power, of energy -- no creator, God, or destiny, no universal rules of good and evil, right and wrong.

That one notion of the Universe neither conspiring for or against me, freed me. What if there is no secret destiny I had to uncover? There isn't a list of right and wrong dictated by some divine order? Could it be so simple? I am alive in an active, moving, undulating world? Karma translates into action or movement. The world acts. You act. You and the world move together. This concept felt straight forward. I imagined a Universe of different courses of action that overlapped, rather than trains running on pre-organized paths. This was a critical perspective shift, and it resonated. It was refreshing and, for the first time in my Life, felt viscerally authentic. My Body and my mind felt in sync. It removed the exhaustive and subjective moral questions and replaced them with pragmatic ones:

- How do you want to act in the world consciously - knowing that there is no right or predestined way to work?
- Every action has a reaction. What was the reaction?
- Where are you now?
- What resources do you have?
- Back to the first question: How do you want to act in the world consciously?

Of course, this concept also expresses the idea that everything is allowed -- your worst nightmares and best dreams. People are free to do as they choose. That is downright frightening. It also just made sense to me. It made room for all the good and bad to be possible simultaneously. There was no *right* or *wrong* move. There are just moves with consequences we cannot predict. As stated so beautifully in the Bhagavad Gita 2.13,[10] "Your entitlement is only to the rite, not ever at all to its fruits." Brooks crystallized this idea in the phrase, "There is only action and even inaction is a form of action."

Furthermore, included in the idea of a power-based Universe was the release of some hidden meaning.

As Douglas's teacher Appa[11] said, "Your Life has no meaning, no purpose, no goal and those are all very good things -- the rest is up to you." When we dispel the need to seek enlightenment as something other than our experience, we affirm the validity of our experience. We make meaning up afterward, and meaning varies based on what you have been indoctrinated to believe or what you have consciously decided to believe. Think about it. What do you define as beautiful? What do you define as strength? Pretty quickly, you will see that we do not share the same meaning of, well, anything.

Yoga empowered me to claim my capacity and urged me to research and own my definitions, meaning and differences. It invited me to be conscious in the way I engaged with everything. It gave me a new pair of glasses through which to see the world. I no longer needed to try to assume or fight against the familiar story of the Judeo-Christian, Western-Capitalist society. I felt like I was flying in the face of the prevailing narrative. I felt like the characters of all those books I had read. They were finding their way, and so was I. I did not scream out this new realization. I held it with me and found ways to interpose myself within what everyone else thought. I found it fun to engage in the world *and* my contrarian inner conversation. I was happy, and still am, to have something that felt right to me.

This f e e l i n g Body of mine became my anchor once again. Instead of running away from the tidal waves of sensations, I turned toward them. The first two years of learning meditation included flashbacks of my rape. Somewhere, along with it all, I trusted in my Body and its expression. Not because I was this enlightened being who knew that it would all fade away. I kept showing up out of cluelessness. I thought I had no other options. And yet, one day, no more flashbacks, and that was interesting to me. It was empowering to me to see myself through a situation that was out of my control. As it were, my Body needed to see it enough to integrate it.

When I was no longer busy trying to fit into some universal paradigm, I began to receive the fullness of my experience in the world. My Body once again reclaimed the title as a friend, not an enemy. Yoga gave me the reflection that my Body was my point of orientation. That love of Self that I knew so deeply as a child was okay to trust indefinitely. The hardest betrayals are the moments I did not listen to my Body's warnings for care. Whether we are conscious or not, the Body has a will to live. It will protect you through pain; it will shut down even when you ignore its cues to rest. Even when I chose self-destructive behavior, it would do everything it could to heal me with the resources that it had. Still, there is always a limit.

The more I settled into the Yoga world, the more strange the world of Dance felt. Yoga birthed a conscious and caring relationship to my Body, and Dance seemed to work against this. Now, don't get me wrong, I did initially repeat the destructive patterns of my dance career, but now with Yoga poses. Even so, I was finding a new way with the shapes. It just took me time to learn. In time, patterns shift. We are what we do the most. Fortunately for me, Yoga became my job, so it forced me to be there, and the gift of that responsibility is the byproduct of its support. Every day I showed up and heard[12] the same messages again and again: "Your Life is a gift," "You are a success just by being born." My brain built new pathways of thinking, and in time the way I interacted with my Body also began to change.

Yoga shifted my relationship to my Body. It reminded me that my Body has always been my anchor, my focus, my compass. This becomes imperative as I continue forward in the world of Yoga. The type of Yoga that I learned gave me a basis for receiving my Body. I met my most influential teachers and it offered me a path of movement that I am still on today. So much of it was good, great even.

However, in 2012 the Anusara method[13] endured a significant breakdown. The founder of the system, John Friend[14], rose in fame, greed and traumatic manipulation. His scandals affected the organization radically. When it fell apart, I decided to drop my affiliation with the organization. I asked myself a critical question, if I was no longer teaching Yoga based on a method, what is my foundation? Where do I start? What is my viewpoint? These questions have taken me years to answer, even though the answer seems obvious now. It's the Body of course. I knew the Body could serve as my anchor, but could it also work well for others?

Biology, the structures and physiological systems offer a guidebook. We can follow stories of pressure (think varicose veins and bigger bones) and dormancy (like cardiovascular disease) in our Bodies. We can see the effects of repeated movements. Our Body presents terms of use, expressing limit through pain. And the more I studied how the Body worked, the more I felt confident that the Body is a perfect starting point to teach Yoga. The Body held together my intuitive relationship with my younger Self and my expanded perspective Self through Yoga.

The more I taught Yoga, the more I conferred with the Body for rule sets and patterns. The more I taught people to be Yoga teachers, the more I trusted the Body to be our foundational resource. I did not want to create the OMNI method of Yoga. Who am I? All universal answers fail and no idea is an original thought. Universal answers are not sophisticated enough to match the gorgeous complexity of Life. And every thought I have thought has been thought before. Life demands paradox, many (seemingly) contradictory things true at the same time. It moves and changes, and sometimes something works here and not there. It is spontaneous and patterned simultaneously.

The Body gives us endless examples of how the many parts of us are necessary. All sensation is allowed. All the difference between the parts is allowed, necessary in fact. I had to learn to recognize the fullness of my feelings, and the Body gave me evidence of how all of you can work together. The Body presents an emergent strategy to engage Life. Differences allowed and IN RELATIONSHIP with each other for the common goal of continuity. America, are you listening? Difference in conscious relationship, not homogeneity, not one country under one God. The Body invites us to see symbiosis and reciprocity of difference. Singularity and unity were the visions of the Nazis. A singular-minded community is a cult. The Body has a much better set of principles to learn from.

To say it explicitly: I am biologically based. I turn toward my Body experience for information and insight to participate in the world around me. I trust in my Body and will to live. I also trust in other Bodies, like yours, and its intention to live. Living is full of questions, and we all will find ways to make meaningful connections. We all have Bodies, and for me, that is a solid starting point. Our Bodies seem to have some inherent understanding of living. So through my Life, I have learned through the lens of my Body. I'm sticking with it. As for the big questions:

Why am I here?

I still don't know.

What is the point of all of this?

Who knows?

What am I supposed to be doing?

Whatever I am doing.

Your turn:

Why am I here?

What is the point of all of this?

What am I supposed to be doing?

2: Reclaim Movement

I promised I would come back to you
I am here now
Can you see me?

Your name
A lexicalized sound
Never stopped calling me home to your sweet
fecund ground

The ah sound emanated from the back of my throat
The uh sound resonated in my belly
The mmm sound vibrated from my mouth

Mama, Mater, Amma, Mutter, Mum, Mother
Mother
Mother
Mother

You are the matrix
The birthplace of Life itself
You have room for us; you give us a place to be our
Bodies

Even when we turn on you

Even when you watch us flail
You root for us
You rise for us
You endure with us
All the while singing your song of Life
Through our blood
Through our tears
Through our milk
Our excess
Our waste

You never abandon us
And you give because you know the endless wealth
of Life itself

You live for us
Like I live for my children
Like I live for ice cream
and the top of my inner thighs

You are not afraid of your big Body
Because it is the source of everything
How do you hate the source of your Life?

And when we are ready
We see you
as you have always been

Sitting back with your legs relaxed
With your feet soft and heavy into the ground you
built

We see you
Your smiling eyes that tell us,
Do as you wish, sweet one

We see you finally and call your name as
we cry and say the words you have told us,
I live for you
I live for you

. . .

A long time ago,

a cell ate another cell. Instead of dying, the cell
inside of the other cell lived and in that one
instance, the birth of complex Life on this planet
was born. Single-celled entities gave way to
multicellular organisms, then plants and animals,
and then advanced thinking human animals like
ourselves.

The potential for Life on Earth is a long story of happenstance, collision, and ironic combination, or so it appears.[1] Two planets collided to create the perfect tilt of our planet, water came to Earth by way of a cosmic storm and our Sun just happened to rest at the perfect goldilocks distance away. It is as cool and sci-fi as it gets. All of these elements came together to allow Life as we know it. Macro thinking is my guilty pleasure.

We love to see ourselves as the top of the food chain. We BE powerful (doing my best George of the jungle impression). But how did we get here and what have we lost and gained along the way? How did we move from animals amongst other animals to where we are now? How were we once swinging through trees and now we Netflix and chill?

We evolved over time to get here. We made quickfire decisions with shortsighted visions. We were trying to survive -- the next moment, next day, next month. We have not always been at the top of the food chain. We, in fact, ranked lower than the hyenas. The lions would eat, then the hyenas, and then we would come in and break open the bones of carcasses and suck out the bone marrow.[2] Gross?

Maybe. Also why bone broth is so very good for our digestive system.

We were also nomadic clan-like people. We climbed trees, hunted and gathered. The entire family/tribe moved together, traveling as needed to weather environmental challenges. Finding food and shelter was a priority. We were MOVERS. Once safety and nourishment were procured, then there was probably time for rest. We only carried what we needed and could carry. So what sparked our transformation? Pun intended -- Fire.

Scientists argue evidence of the first fire between 400,000 and 1.7 million years ago. When we figured out how to make a fire we had a new power and control. Fire allowed us to cook our food or burn down a whole forest. Cooking food aided in the digestive processes and allowed for easier absorption of the nutrients from the food. Apes chew on the same thing for hours to reap the nutrients from the food. Cooking eliminated the need for that.

Cooking = better absorption = better Body metabolism = bigger brains.

Things started to change rapidly. We evolved so fast that the food chain could not keep up with us. We lost the natural order of checks and balances. Besides Mother Earth, nothing could keep us accountable. Imagine a 14 year old with the privileges of a 40 year old -- impulsive, reckless, innovative but, short-sighted. *Bad news.* The regality of the Lion is equal to the grace of the gazelle. They grew together in a shared game of accountability. We shot off like a firecracker on the fourth of July, stunning and alarming at the same time.

We learned to farm. Maybe those early humans thought, "This is great! We don't have to hunt and gather so much! Freeeeeedom." However, for every action, there is a reaction and what we may not have expected was how planting and cultivating wheat domesticated us. It required us to stay in one place and tend to it, all of the time. It allowed us to thrive and procreate and grow communities, which all seemed like progress. It also increased our population size. The possibility of going back to nomadic clans would also mean sacrificing family members and loved ones. Like the one-way valves of your veins, backflow was not permitted. We moved less.

With farming came the growth of communities, cities, narratives, laws; and this establishes culture. The stories we have told ourselves have been as important as our lived lives. Humans have accomplished *a lot* by just agreeing on a singular story. Who determines this common narrative? Well, the winners have always decided that and the powerful and privileged usually win. That doesn't mean it is fair. Life is not fair -- review Darwin and Brooks' take on the Universe. A power Universe is not a just or moral Universe. Culture brings conflict and cooperation, war and alliance. Culture curates belief systems that systematically create hierarchy, dominance and submission. The acceptance of a common narrative dictates prescribed ways of moving.

Jump ahead to the Industrial Revolution and there is an incredible period of urbanization. Advancement in industrial and mechanical technologies replaced labor-intensive jobs. Again, humans must have thought, "Wow, we have done it this time! Machines! No more work! Freeeeeedom." Action, reaction y'all. A person can *think* they know what will come of their actions, but in reality no one has any idea. Rural life shifted to an urban lifestyle. The new city life generally required less movement compared to country life, consequently decreasing levels of physical activity. The work was repetitive and lacked variability -- working at a machine, sewing buttons on a coat, over and over with the same motions for eight plus hours of the day.

Are you noticing a trend? We are mammals that have cultured ourselves to think that we no longer exist in the natural world. Don't believe me? Here is the definition of nature straight from the Oxford English Dictionary:

na·ture
/ˈnāCHər/
Noun
the phenomena of the physical world collectively, including plants, animals, the landscape, and other features and products of the Earth, <u>as opposed to humans or human creations.</u>

We have literally exempted ourselves from nature. Furthermore, the cost of industrialization and urbanization becomes glaringly apparent in our Bodies starting in the 1950s and 1960s. An epidemic of hypokinetic diseases including cardiovascular disease, cancer, and type II diabetes, never before prevalent, became recognized as the leading causes of illness and death. What does hypokinetic mean? "hypo"=low/ not-enough "kinetic" =movement: NOT ENOUGH MOVEMENT DISEASE.[3] The lifestyle "improvements" brought in part by the Industrial Revolution had come with an unwanted and alarming cost to health, which we still suffer from today.

And now? Here we are, in the midst of a significant new wave of advancement and change that is affecting us dramatically and irreversibly. We are moving further into a world of technology and convenience. We can uber ourselves and our food. We can amazon prime just about anything to our door in a day. The movement it takes to receive something as a consumer takes almost nothing more than a few clicks on an app. The labor on the production side is another story altogether. We drive most places. We walk on paved sidewalks and walk-ways. The COVID-19 pandemic has even fostered a new reason for staying home, for protection and survival.

Movement is dying. Discounting our physicality and prioritizing the mind is #trending.

In Katy Bowman's marvelous book, *Move Your DNA*,[4] she teaches us about the flopped dorsal fin of captive Orcas. In this profound example, she explains that the good news is, there are still Orcas in the wild to compare to the Orcas in captivity. The contrast offers us a space to learn. Orcas in captivity are contained in a small pool. This limits their ability to swim through a variety of different pressures. Orcas in captivity also often have flopped dorsal fins. The dorsal fin is made of dense connective tissue, not bone. As Orcas in the wild swim, they move up and down into varying depths and pressures. They also have room to swim at different speeds. All of this movement in combination with the water's varying pressure makes the fin sturdy.

Now think of fucking sea world. These poor animals swim in circles, able to achieve only a fraction of the biological movement they have in their natural environment. With no pressure and no variability = their fin flops. Pressure is the language of the Body, in Orca Bodies and human Bodies. Pressure influences everything from bone growth to blood.

Bowman continues and notes that animals in captivity suffer from three major things:

- Obesity
- Infertility
- Aggression

It doesn't take too long to infer this metaphor to the human species.

In short, we have created our own captivity. We are the Orcas in our self-made sea world. We are forgetting that we came from the Earth and will go back into it. We are forgetting that we are a part of nature. Our Bodies were built by movement and movement has always been a part of the story of our Bodies -- until now.

Have you seen Moana?[5] Moana longs for the sea, despite her Father's orders to stay put on her island. He urges her that the sea is dangerous, that it is safer on their island. But the sea calls her. Her irreverent grandmother tells her about her past, about their people's past. They were voyagers; partners with the sea. Her grandmother bridges the gap between Moana's deep visceral knowledge with the experience of her ancestors. When Moana learns all of this, she runs out of the cave and screams, "We were VOYAGERS! We can voyage again!"

Early humans stood up on two legs around 3.9-4.2 million years ago. Homosapapiens lived as movers for the majority of our species-hood. In the last 10,000 years, we have cultivated domestication and sedentarism. There is a mismatch[6] between the evolution of our biology and the evolution of our cultured living circumstances. We were MOVERS! We can move again.

To understand how movement influences our health, we must understand the word: **Mechanotransduction.** Mechano + Transduction = any of the various mechanisms by which cells convert mechanical stimuli into electrochemical activity. This form of sensory transduction/conversion is responsible for several neural and physiological processes in the Body, including proprioception, touch, balance, and hearing. The primary mechanism of mechanotransduction involves converting mechanical signals into electrical or chemical signals.

Simplified -- The Mechanical World is everything outside of you. Not you. As it (the Mechanical World) touches, presses, pushes, affects you, your Body converts that information into chemical and electrical communication. Your nervous system assimilates that information and dictates a response. Mechanotransduction describes the ongoing process by which you and the World around you are in a relationship. You are *never-not* in a relationship with the World. We are inextricably woven into the World and born from it.

Now bring this back to our evolution as a species. We evolved as Movers. Now even though we have stopped moving, our genome is still programmed as model "hunter-gatherer." Therefore, if you want health in this "hunter-gatherer" Body of yours, then you need movement. Movement is as essential to our lives as water, food, and air. Say it with me:

Movement is essential to my Life.
Movement is essential to my Life.
Movement is essential to my Life.

One primary key to health is just moving on an everyday basis. To be clear, moving is different from exercise and also includes it. Moving describes taking all your Body parts through space and time in all ranges of motion in varying degrees of action. Exercise can be a term that just describes "leg day" at the gym. Moving as essential to living is an understanding that is void from our educational system. Why? Because, again, we took ourselves out of nature. If there is a fall from Grace, this is it. We have intellectually extricated ourselves from the very thing that birthed us.

In education, we have programmed gym class once a week, recess on nice days only, thirty-minute quick-ab workouts and hot pockets. The common narrative is brainwashing us to believe that technology and mediocrity is the goal. The irony is not lost on me, that we have also evolved enough that I can write my thoughts out on this page to share with you. Our reclamation story is remembering.

Our work is retrofitting the truth that WE WERE MOVERS, we can move again! I am not suggesting that we all leave our homes and retreat to mountains and caves. We have the invitation to find the space between where we are and where we have been. Where we are and where we are going.

We must come back to our Bodies. We must learn about them in first person language, not objectification. Think about it. When did you learn about your Body? Was it a silly song in Kindergarten? Do you remember 10th grade biology and what you learned in that class? Was it a pamphlet about puberty or those 1970s books like *What's Happening to Me*? What was your very first impression/experience when thinking about the Body? Now, think about your relationship with your Body.

Are you friends?
Sworn enemies?
Do you feel like your Body "has your back" or has it let you down?

How do you relate to your human Body experience? I have taught enough people to report back and say that the going trend I see is disassociation, dissatisfaction and even betrayal. A few years back, I went back to school to begin pre-med prerequisites and as one of the oldest folks in the room, I was struck by one major thing:

We learn about the Body in processes of objectification.

THE Kidneys, not MY Kidneys.
THE Heart, not MY Heart.
THE Respiratory System, not MY Respiratory
System.

When we learn about ourselves in a disassociated
way, we embed disassociation. Furthermore,
English is a noun-based language, which means, we
describe everything as things/objects. Nouns flatten
the action/connection of the object it represents.
English strips away the Life of the object for a
facade of what once was there.

English is also the language of the colonizer. On
the contrary, Indigenous languages are often
verb-based. Meaning that the word that describes
something is actually a description of what that
thing does. For example, instead of "fork", it might
be "food picker-upper." In this way, verb-based
languages preserve the Life energy of the object.
And this matters because when we learn through
connection, we develop that connection.

The western education system is objectification at
its best. Separate everything out, study it, dissect it

-- rip it from the whole. It is explicit and discounts the fecundity.

Is there any saving grace? Consciousness is key. If you can see the system for what it is, you can engage with it. Fill in the gaps, reclaim the past that has been stripped away and hidden. Stay alert. Narrative has been one way for our species to survive, but it has also come with manipulation and consequence. The story we choose is important. We must reclaim, reshape, rewrite our story.

I suggest that we study the Body AS ourselves. As I studied more about THE Body, I began to replace THE Body with MY Body. I worked to restore the living, moving, essence of all these parts that I was studying. It takes a muscular engagement to re-hitch nouns back to their aliveness, but it can be done. We can recall the felt sense behind the lifeless nouns and re-forge their connection. Wanna try?

Think of your favorite throw pillow.
Where did you get it?
How much was it?
How many hours of work did you have to do to afford it?

Where is it now?
What room?
Do you even use it?
What color is it?
What fabric is it made out of?
How was that fabric made?
Who made it?

As you ask yourself each of these questions, you simultaneously cull up sensation. Your whole Body remembers and connects you to the object. Each question envelops you with the Life embedded in the object.

If we learned about our Bodies as OUR BODIES we might also feel more empowered to sustain our health. If you learn about the Body as an object, there is no personal tie or agency to keep it well. Agency feels foreign. If we own the context of our experience, we get to know our baselines and our "normal" so that when something is amiss, we might also know the difference.

People are living longer, and yet they are also living with chronic pain. There is an opioid crisis. Our entire medical system is oriented around stopping pain, not about connecting to it. Pain is always protective. Pain is **always** preempted by a loss of stability and safety. Pain is your best friend. It keeps you safe, even when you don't know you need to. Pain is a complex expression of your entire Life, a concoction of biology, psychology, and sociology. Pain is a conversation to be had, not ignored.

The sensations of your Body are evidence of your aliveness. To feel your Life is to remember that you are *never-not* a part of nature and the wondrous backstory of this strange rock. You are also the mistakes and technological advances that allow for poverty, injustice and pandemics. We are all of our stories -- Reclaim them, re-make them. Connect back to connection. As we re-cognize our place in nature we receive the Grace of being alive.

3: Holding Life

I wrote this to you while you were sleeping
As I watched guard over your breath
As I counted the beats of your heart.

I am not in control
I am just a pattern keeper
An intuit through whom you came
I am your star charter.

I wrote this in the moonlight of the winter solstice,
In the dark of your room
To the sounds of your congestion.

I could not see the page as I wrote this
So it made me write slow
I had to *feel* the words as I etched each one onto the
page
I double checked the words by tracing them with
my fingertips.

These words are whispers
Straight from the moon to my brain
Or is it my brain to the moon?

Motherhood is a rush towards madness
And I must keep remembering how big I am.
Big enough to hold madness like a small bug under
a cup
Buzzing all around but
Contained within.

While you sleep
I'll hold space for you
I will try to see what you might not know yet
But I won't tell you until you ask.
Because help, when it is not asked for, is not
helping.

Or maybe it is?
Am I just afraid?

This period of time is marked by hyper-vigilance
And vigilance it will be
Moon by moon,
Until you say no more
Or until I remember you have your own work to do
and I can only be near you while you do it.

Then, and only then
Will I go sit down and watch my own breath again
Will I listen to the birds again

And my wartime attention will fade back into creativity.

• • •

Motherhood has tested my appreciation for my own story.

I was the kid who loved playing with dolls. I requested the *real* ones with the *real parts.* My first job was as a Mother's helper when I was 10. She paid me a dollar an hour. I watched a 10 month old while the Mother slept on the couch. When I asked for two dollars an hour, she said, "I can find someone else."

Despite losing my first gig, I went on to be an excellent babysitter. I loved hanging out with kids -- I was a natural. My first dance teaching job was on Saturday mornings at a YWCA with thirty-three 3 year olds. All. By. Myself. I guess they didn't think an 18 year old would mind handling thirty-three toddlers without an assistant, a vote of confidence mixed with exploitation. I was like a Mother goose with thirty-three goslings. They were my little army of creative dance munchkins. I organized that class with assigned spots and line-order. It was actually one of my favorite parts of the week and despite the numbers, I was really good at my job.

I always knew I wanted to be a Mother. I imagined myself having two boys and feeling great. When I met my husband-to-be, I was on the tail-end of my Life imploding and crumbling before me. My job at the Yoga studio was not working. I was reverse commuting from NYC to NJ every day to open the studio at 8 am. I woke up at 5 am every morning to do this. My favorite part was buying coffee and this croissant filled with cotija cheese at the corner bakery. I still dream about that croissant. I was running the studio and wondering at 26, what the heck am I doing with my Life? I had been dancing and working with one dance company since I was 18 and was questioning that too. I was also living through the dissolution of a long term relationship with my then wife, well domestic partnership, because same-sex marriage was not legal yet. I met my former wife at a messy 19. Seven years later, I was a messy 26. In the span of a month, I was both fired/quit from the Yoga studio and left the dance company I had been a part of for eight years. In turn, my wife had left me for another woman and I basically crumbled into a pile of mush. I, in fact,

was actually slumped on a corner in Queens crying
on the phone to my Father, whining out the words:
Whaaaaat ammm I gonnnnna dooooohoooohooo?

After my wife left, I ran wild. I spent that summer
in the city staying out night after night. I avoided
reality as hard as I could. I ran out of money and
after being out on my own since 21, I came home. I
allowed myself to be submerged in my breaking
down. I needed work and although a restaurant in
Jersey City offered me work five days a week, I
turned it down. I took a job closer to my parents'
home that offered me two shifts a week. It was
probably one of the kindest moves I have ever made
for myself. I was tired and I actually listened to my
Body and let it slowly recover.

I was trained by this *guy*, Daryl. He was aloof and
handsome and, a year later, we were married. A few
months later, Vishali told me that she was trying to
sell the Yoga studio. One of the reasons I left the
studio in the first place was to just feel free. The
studio demanded daily responsibility, and at 26, I
wasn't sure I was ready to feel beholden to the
studio for my whole Life. When I met Daryl we
could barely wait to have children. The thought of
having my own family was exciting to me. I knew

what the studio required. Both a family and the studio needed me to be there for them. At that moment, I felt ready to be there for both.

We took over the Yoga studio and six months later, I got pregnant. I was elated. I could not wait to be the incredible Mother I thought I would be. I talked about all the things I would teach them and all the organic baby food purees I would make. Naivete at its best. I had *some* understanding, so I thought I knew it all. I now love hearing expecting parents talk about what they *plan* on doing. So cute. I know exactly where they are, and I dare not burst their bubble. We learn when we learn.

The journey of pregnancy began. We find out that we are having a girl. I am shocked, excited but shocked. Pregnancy is a time when you have the unique job of being a container -- the fetus shares your food, your resources, your Life. I like to say you are *holding* Life rather than creating Life. *Life creates Life.* Remember the story about a cell eating another cell? It's like that, Life inside of Life -- both self-sustaining *and* in relationship. As I see it, it continues like this when they are Earthside. My children are their own beings who made it through my Body. I hold space for their Life, I am their guardian, not their creator.

Pregnancy is often marketed as this precious time when the Mother is glowing and radiant. If you have felt like this, congratulations. You are in the minority. Pregnancy was hard for me. It felt like an alien was stealing all of my resources and I was still expected to perform as I normally would. We need to hire a new marketing firm for the journey of pregnancy. One that includes the tumult of the actual experience. We need to rewrite the narrative and include the reality of it.

The joys of my first pregnancy included visual migraines every day for the first three months. I would lose my eyesight in the right eye and then the left. My left arm would feel disassociated from my Body like it was not my arm. My gums bled, I had rhinitis (stuffy nose), and a hemorrhoid that had such a presence, my husband named it *dingleberry*. I also had so much fear. I remember being perplexed about how I was going to get this baby out of me. It just didn't seem possible.

Her birth was pretty medicalized due to my lack of information. I was induced because my OB was going on vacation. The doctor broke my water and I was given Pitocin. Pitocin is a synthetic hormone that actually works on the same receptors as oxytocin. This means that Pitocin blocks oxytocin. Oxytocin aka *the love hormone* helps the Body in both the process of expelling the baby, as well as mitigating the intensity of the pain. It is a super hormone. However, instead of feeling the love drug, Pitocin made my contractions feel like someone was repeatedly stabbing me in the belly and twisting the knife. There was no love happening. I was having piggie-back contractions and in a decision to not let my first Birth feel like a trauma, I asked for an epidural. That shit is strong, so strong, in fact, that I agreed to watch Rachel Ray on the cooking channel. #terrible

The epidural made it almost impossible to feel my vagina as I pushed, so I pushed way too hard during delivery and had to do months of pelvic floor rehab postpartum. But, in a moment of true bliss, there she was. There she was. When I saw her for the first time, I felt so proud of my Body for what it had accomplished and so excited to meet this new little being. I just kept saying, Hi, hi, HI, hiiiii, Hi.

Now, I was a Mom. Just like that. It was an abrupt transition. I was now in charge of keeping that cell who lived inside of me alive, outside of me. The nice thing about pregnancy is that your Body knows what to do. When they are here now, separate from you, you begin this cognitive dance of panic and hypervigilance. It is a 24-hour-a-day job, 7-days-a-week, with little to no reprieve. Add exhaustion to all of this and you have one hell of a concoction. This type of exhaustion cannot be explained, only experienced. It was a level of torture at times. No amount of caffeine could help. I sunk into a trench of tiredness and would pray that people would just show up with lasagna at my door. I'd wishfully talk to friends about starting a commune and going back to the Life of hunter-gatherers. I look disheveled -- really Earthy.

Then there was breastfeeding. I was unaware and uninformed and suffered through with mashed and bleeding nipples because of an undiagnosed tongue tie. Every two hours, I would set up to breastfeed, help my daughter latch, and then brace myself on the arms of the rocking chair as she would pull milk from breasts. It was the sharpest pain for the first 30 seconds, like blades coming through my most sacred parts. I was willful and should have given up or asked for more help, but I didn't.

Juxtaposed with the pain, was the sweetest touch my Body has ever felt. Her fingers tracing my forearms and her little eyes on me could just melt me into a puddle. I was in love with Isla despite my own personal Body experience. The ardor didn't compromise the well of happiness within me. It was all happening at once. We are born in the middle of other people's lives. It is all happening at once. Before you enter the world, the momentum of your parents' actions has been turning for years. We are all born right into it. My experience was commingled with hers. To be with my new light beam was breathtaking and heart-making.

My husband started a new job during this time. He began to work 60+ hours a week and I went back to work just one month after the birth of our daughter. Survival became our normal. Both of us were fighting for a sense of normalcy. We started to lose sight of each other. At around 10 months after Isla's birth, we were teetering on a dangerous edge. We were unraveling. We were financially strapped and trying so hard to just make ends meet. Some people have enough resources to not feel such intensity in parenting. They can hire night nurses and nannies. When you are poor and young, you just figure shit out. We kept figuring it out.

As if Life was not full enough, we took on more. We bought a second Yoga studio because we thought that was a good idea (worst idea). I became pregnant again. This pregnancy began with twenty straight weeks of nausea, followed by a separated pubic symphysis. I couldn't move my feet more than six inches apart without excruciating pain. No asymmetrical movement for weeks which meant no Yoga. Because I could barely move, I gained extra weight and needed to have pelvic floor physical therapy. My Body felt miserable. The day before I gave birth, I looked like I might murder someone and I know that because a friend told me afterward she was scared for her Life.

We had prepared for this birth. We had a birth coach who was brilliant.[1] I had a friend as a doula. I was determined to birth naturally and without any interventions. I was ready. I also didn't know exactly what to expect because my first birth was rushed. The night before I went into labor, I felt deep and heavy cramping. It was primal and vulnerable and I just kept giving into it. Like waves at the shoreline, I let them wash over me. My feeling Body lulled me into a birth that felt like the best meditation I have ever had. My second birth was magical -- my Body produced amazing hormones to ease pain, my Body involuntary pushed for me. I had a true physiological birth, no interventions and the natural timing of my Body in tandem with Willa's. Willa felt like birthing a tornado. She came with a powerful force and was born "en caul" which means she crowned in her amniotic sac. This is a once in an 880,000 chance. I was once again elated.

With my second birth, I was determined to use my time in the hospital well. I was going to sleep more before we had to go home. I learned from Isla just how tired I was about to become. That first night, I could barely sleep. I had asked the nurses to watch Willa in the nursery and within about an hour, they brought her back. The nurse said, "Honey, we can't get her to stop crying, your turn." Willa nursed for almost 3 hours straight. I had to ask the nurses for a pacifier, which as a first-time Mother I would have never asked for, but she was fed and still wanting to suck. My elation started to turn toward worry.

We came home and the next three months became dark. By day three with Willa, I was losing ground. My mood was down, way down. Willa was sad and hungry and having a hard time. Willa had colic and was generally unhappy most of the time. Her cry was like a blow horn. Isla's cry sounded like a little whimper compared to the lungs on this kid. I can vividly remember Isla bouncing one of her dolls on her shoulder (mimicking me with Willa) saying, "it's okay, it's okay, please stop crying."

Willa also had a tongue tie and I was overproducing milk, so every feeding was like a garden hosing to her face. I did what I could to seek out help, but managing yourself when you are at your lowest is hard. It is very easy to lose your way in Motherhood. Postpartum depression is an insidious snake. In the isolation, everything felt like it was closing down around me. I could not find any perspective, any room to see myself. I kept thinking to myself, am I crazy or is this just how demanding it is? To watch Willa suffer and feel helpless was heart-wrenching, gut-ripping. I can still feel her cries. I needed more support, I needed my Mother so that I could Mother. American culture promotes the message that the new family needs privacy to become a unit. However, I would argue that it is that isolation that leads to such a high postpartum depression rate. I am now a Doula and what I have learned is that in many cultures, birth is not experienced as a stressful time. In many African cultures, Mothers and Fathers feel revered and cared for during this time. This is possible due to the immediate and continuous support of the family from their community. American culture works on isolation and independence and I believe this is also why we are so dysfunctional. Mothers need so much more support.

As a first-world country, we have one of the worst Maternal, Fetal, and Infant Mortality Rates.[2] That says a lot about a country when its most vulnerable populations are dying. It is also radically disproportionate. BIPOC Mothers are 3-4 times more likely to have a negative birth outcome. The main reason for this is systemic racism and the dismissive practices of the medical industry towards BIPOC women and their health. The extra burden of systemic and systematic racism, microaggressions, and discrimination based on white supremacy is devastating. So devastating, in fact, that it only takes one generation of living in America for BIPOC women to have the same 3-4x increase in negative birth outcomes. Even if generations of their family lived elsewhere, the discrimination and stress based on race are so strong, so prevalent, it only takes one generation to shift the outcomes.

We must continue to break down the common narrative and move toward equity. As a doula, my main desire is to advocate for Women in these incredibly intense times. If I can provide stress relief for Mothers and help increase their chance for positive birth outcomes, that will be something. The Medical World is the Patriarchy. Did you know that the reason Women birth on their backs is because the French King Louis XIV (1637-1709) insisted on watching Woman's vulva as they gave birth? He couldn't see well enough so he had the birthing table created, equipped with stirrups. Four hundred years later and we are still birthing this way, despite the vast research available about more optimal birthing positions. We must keep acknowledging the traumas of our past so that we can move forward coherently. We can do this by learning about the past and decolonizing our own minds and assumptions.

Because there is not enough support for Mothers, I remember slipping into a fog and just thinking to myself, this is what Motherhood is, you have no choice. I did not ask for help -- I willed myself through despair. As many Mothers do. I went back to work too early. I was hopeless and dissociated. My husband picked up where I couldn't. He held so many spaces. He was the only one who could calm Willa and get her to sleep for the entire first year of her Life.

And then just like someone turned on the light, Willa stopped crying and she started laughing. Her laugh was as loud as her cry and it was epic. I bathed in her laughter. It was contagious and like a rainbow after a crazy thunderstorm. At this moment, many months after her birth, we began to bond. The despair seemed to melt away and the embrace of Love took over.

Motherhood has tested my appreciation for my own story.

Even as a Mother of two incredible children, I felt like an imposter. I have never been impressed by my version of Mother. There is so much I wish I could just rewind and do-over. But I can't. Motherhood has broken me down and made me question just about everything. I have a deep trust in my relationship with my Body, but deep trust in relationship to their Bodies? No, not yet. I am still always, *always* learning. I have felt such a wide gamut of emotions. I have absolutely visited madness, regularly. It is hard to come back some days.

Have you ever chanted Aum at the beginning of Yoga class? This sound is a representation of the possibility and eternality of the entire Universe. The A is the part before sound emerges when you open your mouth and take a deep breath in. It is also the beginning of things -- creation. The U is the point where the mouth is half-open and half-closed with the lips softly pursed. This part describes the work of sustenance, of holding the sound, holding the Life created. The M completes the cycle. It is made by bringing your lips together and finalizing the sound. It symbolizes the inevitable dissolution of all things. This sound includes everything. Motherhood includes everything. It is a very vivid ride of creation, sustenance, and dissolution. Over and over again.

Sometimes you create milk, sometimes you create pain.

Sometimes you sustain nourishment, sometimes you sustain loss.
Sometimes you dissolve fear, sometimes you dissolve the version of yourself you thought you would be.
Endless cycles -- each of them proof of your aliveness.

I have had to learn to surrender to the cycles of this process called Motherhood. I have had to get so frustrated that the wall I was banging my head up against became the same wall I eventually turned around and rested into. I have had to trust and practice my connection to something bigger than myself. I have had to close my eyes and just pray to the moon so that I could soften the unreasonable blows. Motherhood, like the effacing of the cervix at birth, feels like a slow and gradual thinning, creating surges of pressure to forge a pathway for Life to be born. I may have birthed my children but Motherhood has birthed me too.

And then there is Lil.

Lil was our wrench, our surprise baby. The timing of her unexpected pregnancy came at an already uncertain time. Our second business was failing and draining the resources of our flagship studio. We were drowning in debt and the busy work of raising a family. My husband and I were like passing ships. I would work the morning shift and then pass the torch to him for the afternoon. I had gained momentum in a cycle of overworking. My visions were set on survival. Did I mention we were drowning? I was terrified and I was treading water every hour of the day. I began to deprioritize basic human needs. I was like a whirlwind, full of energy and destruction. I felt like I had no other choice but to sink or swim, so I was swimming. The health of our marriage was deteriorating.

Every month I thought I was pregnant. And every month Daryl would go buy me a pregnancy test and it would be negative. Every month except for one. We were both frozen in disbelief. Isla was almost 7 and Willa 5. We had just achieved the next parental milestone -- both kids were in school. Now, we were being hurled back into the baby years, where the physical and emotional toll is a high price to pay. We were already barely making it. As it turns out, this news of this pregnancy would send us into a tailspin.

Here was another moment in my Life where the ground seemed to give way -- reminiscent of that moment when I was in a ball on the street in Queens. In these moments, the floor crumbles beneath me and I feel myself fall all the way down. It was a ball pit moment. As Lil grew inside of me, our marriage fell apart. Daryl left us in what seemed like a spontaneous decision. I had felt him withdrawing ever since I decided to keep the baby. But I just thought to myself, he will get over it. He didn't.

I found myself pregnant with our third child and losing my husband. We all felt loss and trauma. I remember talking to Isla about her feelings and she said, "What is this? This thing I feel?" I answered it is loss. I told her that she had the capacity for this moment. She then asked me when I first learned about loss. The truth was that I was learning it the hardest at that moment alongside her. So I told her, now, with you. She replied, "How come you are so old and I am learning so young?" I answered, I don't know, there is no reason for that.

Willa was still pretty pre-verbal, so I just watched her trying to internalize the loss of her favorite person in the world. It was an ambiguous loss, because he was gone, but not gone. Whether we know it is coming or it hits us unaware, loss will affect us all. Then, in a moment, we are changed, it marks us and becomes a part of our story.

As I traversed through the work of the world, the internal work of growing Miss Lillian felt quiet. I distinctly remember telling my Body, just handle it. I created this division between my mind and my Body. I was living in stress, barely sleeping, taking no prenatal vitamins and running on empty. I was trying to be strong for Isla and Willa. I told myself that there was no room for me right now.

As the weeks went on, Daryl fell deeper into a hole. He was uncharacteristically himself. I was furious with him and yet still concerned. It felt like we were rocks rolling down a hill, side by side and yet I could not stop his momentum or trajectory. I could see him about to crash. I even tried to scream and warn him, but I knew that the crash was coming and would eventually happen anyway. I was right. I knew it in my Body and that truth was palpable. I uncovered the truth that he was having an affair.

My heart broke.

A few days later, I was served with papers suing us for defaulting on the loan for our second Yoga studio. I sold my wedding rings for cash to feed the kids and began to move toward divorce. I saw a few divorce lawyers who basically all told me the same thing, "Divorce is for rich people and you are not rich. Come to an agreement."

I knew there was no way of avoiding him. He was the Father of my two, almost three girls, so I prepared myself. I shoved my emotions as far down as I could, I went into hypervigilance and pragmatic Omni mode and I tasked out the work.

But, paradoxically, there was also this funny feeling inside of me. I kept thinking to myself, *this* must be real Love. I hated him with all my being and yet I couldn't help but feel for him. He took a hard fall. He threw away his most important beings. He was hurting. As his wife, I was betrayed, but as his best friend, I had compassion for him. Everyone was on my side and he really had no one. Life is not fair, but it is real. We all make mistakes. I saw his humanity and I saw mine. I was also hoping that the Father of my children was okay. And, that felt like real Love, different than I had ever known before.

My friend said to me, "I'm curious to see how you will handle this."[3] In that statement, she gave me permission to not know. She reminded me that wonder is an adult tool. I curiously allowed space for the next steps to become clear. I began to just talk with Daryl again. We had no choice but to move through our debris. So we did.

In the midst of this new work, I had a TIA, a Transient Ischemic Attack, which was an emergent outcome from the stress I was under. I couldn't read words, or remember Willa's name. I was disoriented and had tingling in my left arm and tongue. It was the scariest moment of my Life. My go-to emergency contact, Daryl, was not living with us, so Isla had to talk to 911 and get the ambulance to our house. Willa and Isla rode to the hospital with me. I called Daryl and he joined us. We all just cried and these tears helped us process. The course back to each other began coming into view.

At eight months, I started to feel safe enough to consciously connect with the Baby inside of me. I had told my Body to keep guard, but I had not allowed myself to feel her beautiful force inside of me. I was losing everything; I didn't want to lose her as well.

We often call Lil, our phoenix, as she seemed to emerge from it all unscathed and yet from a Body perspective, she was in it along with us all. We think of the womb as this sterile protected space -- and it is to some extent. However, this world is filled with pressure and she and I shared resources. She is made from me and her Father. She holds this pressure too. None of which is her fault, but influenced nonetheless. Lineage supports us and burdens us. We all must find a way to emerge.

In the last month before Lil arrives, Daryl and I work to mend our family. We choose each other again. I choose him, again. Not out of fear and lack, but out of resilience. Daryl openly wore his scarlet letter. To this day, he continues to build back our trust. He is a courageous man to face his mistakes and do the work of repair. This is our ongoing marriage story -- *Our Life as Five*. This tumultuous time filled with great loss has also allowed for great growth in my family. The Love that has come from this place of incredible despair and breakdown is the very beginning of real strength.

We decided to shut down our second Yoga studio and cut our losses. We made our family the priority and we prepared ourselves for Lillian's Earthbound entrance. Lillian's birth was scary and fast. I was worried and just wanted safety for us all. Lil made it, with a cord around her neck two times, but she was here, welcomed by us both. Thrice I was elated.

Motherhood has tested my appreciation for my own story.

The bumps along the way have left some well-deserved bruises. I have had to relinquish my expectation of what I thought I would be like as a Mother; to fully receive how I am as a Mother. What I know today is that my Body holds my narrative. This beautiful Body has expanded and contracted, grown boobs and bellies, endured broken hearts for bigger more spacious ones. It has allowed the pathway for three incredible little women to be born into their own Lives. The journey of that has been nothing short of dramatic and worth every single second. Motherhood has taught me to *keep feeling* through the events of my Life -- because all of it is evidence of my aliveness, of my fullness and my complexity. This is it.

Embedded in my cells is the gorgeous story of us. Woven into the fabric of my being: I can feel Isla and her stunning independence and imagination, I can feel Willa's immense power and light, I can feel Lillian's mischievous and playful soul, I can feel the bond of Daryl's partnership. And I can feel myself, this wise old lady who is so big, she can hold it all. Holding Life has been my privilege and greatest teacher.

I offer my story to you so that you might remember to tell yours. If you are ready and feel safe, listen to your Body's narrative. It might just be one of your favorite stories.

4: Emergence

You are fullness in form
There is nothing you can do that will make Life
abandon you
Open the inner sanctum
And dare to be seen
For just a moment come out of your protections
So you know that you are safe here too

You will be celebrated and held
Enjoy the jostling as everyone shares in your light
And don't forget your trauma
Connect back to your feelings
From times when you had no time
To process the change

Flow back and acknowledge that even birth is a
violent act
What we are not provided
Requires us to rise to our own occasion
You have never been alone
You are the beauty of what Life can be

Delight in your fullness
All parts of you allowed

The hypervigilance
The bird watcher
The pitbull
And the laughing grandMother

And continue into the unresolved future
Shift and dance and glimmer
Move as Life moves us
Mischievously content with it all
Smiling all the way home

•••

It has been a funny thing to trust myself; to listen to
the musings that repeat within me. Sometimes I
pretend I don't hear them, as if they would just
drop it and move on. But, as I am learning, these
musings come from the depth of my self-organizing
magnificence. They are me and do not wish to be
quelled. They will for my Life and that is very very
good news. Some days I am brave enough to just
listen inward, to hear their whispers and howls. On
those days, I bask in my own warmth and glow and
wonder. They might simply say, "this is it" or gently
offer "no" or "yes," but they come with weight.

These musings are heavy with truth and that is how I know to trust them -- to trust myself.

I started writing this book because I thought I might not make it to 40-years-old. In a span of two months, I had experienced forty-seven extreme neurological migraines, each one presenting with stroke-like symptoms. I thought I was dying. Each day was a mixture of panic, fear, abandon, and dissociation. I was walking dead -- still trying to do my jobs as Mother, wife and business owner. I was losing the ability to speak the words I was thinking and losing weight at a fast pace. The level of physical pain and disorientation I was experiencing was harrowing. One night after waking up from a dream that felt like my mind was on the brink of a severe precipice, I began to write down my thoughts. I wanted my girls to know me through my words, in case that is all they had. The computer exacerbated my migraines, but I still wrote feverishly. In looking back at those first drafts, I mixed up words, had unfinished sentences and many, many typos -- typos on words like "the" and "and." My right brain was writing, while my left brain broke down. How did I get there? That is a long story, I have told some parts already. Still...there is always more.

After Lillian was born, it felt like I had received a
boon. Lillian was an easy baby. She had a tongue
tie, just like her sisters. Because of her sisters, I
knew to check for it and had the resources to help.
She had a frenulectomy at 6 weeks, which has its
own violence. The baby is given no pain medicine
and in a *long* 6-10 seconds, the frenulums are cut
with a laser. Then for 2 weeks, I had to stretch
those healing tissues every 4 hours. It was sheer
torture to inflict pain on my newborn. However,
this surgery generally allows the relationship of
breastfeeding to thrive. For us, it did. Breastfeeding
was going well. I even felt like the calmest version
of Mother I had ever been. As a family, we had just
endured and moved through so much that this
window of bliss felt deserved. I was enjoying it and
excited for the future. Daryl and I had started
counseling to actively work on our marriage. The
girls were in therapy as well. I was peacocking,
thinking I had figured it all out.

I had been in a similar situation before and
"handled" it with the same mental escapes. After
my rape, I thought I could process it by just shoving
the experience as far down into my subconscious as
possible. In that instance, when I would start to

think about it, I would just redirect my attention to food. I would think about all the ways I could cut calories or the excuses I would use to explain to my College floormates why I wouldn't be at the food hall, again. I would do tae bo videos three times a day or drink five cups of coffee to keep my mind sharp. All of those tactics worked for a while. Until they didn't. In my early twenties, my Body hit a threshold where it would no longer hold my experience in the background. I went through a two year period where almost every time I closed my eyes, the first thing I would see was the rape. It was disturbing. Until it wasn't. I fought it and resisted, until I didn't. I went to a smattering of therapists but felt like they never helped me access why these flashbacks kept repeating. So I kept at it by myself (which I do not recommend). I didn't feel like I had any other choice and so there came a point where I expected them. The more the memory replayed, the more I could see the complexity of that moment. I allowed myself to feel the pain that I hurried myself away from before. I found moments of compassion for my sweet young self. I would comfort myself by saying -- it's not your fault, how could you have known? In those moments, I felt like I was holding myself. And then one day, the regularity of the flashbacks stopped and when they infrequently played again, the intense physiological charge was not with them.

In this lullaby space of our new family of five, I once again, delusionally thought that I had processed the trauma of the past nine months, fuck it, the past three years. As we welcomed friends and family to meet our new bundle of joy and our renewed partnership, I floated off into the ethers. I was in a full-on oxytocin coma. I was high on Motherhood and my ability to survive the past year.

Willa caught a cold from school. As my new-confident-Mother-of-three-self, I scoffed and thought, even though Lil was young, it's no big deal. I rested on the understanding that the Body is amazing and can heal. I even believed that Lillian would have the best immunity and that these were just third child problems. Lil naturally caught Willa's cold and started to sound congested. I felt prepared to weather this *basic* cold with her.

I was holding a large ceremony at the Yoga studio. One that included my family. This was going to be the first time so many special people would meet Lillian. She was an easy baby who didn't mind being held by others, something that neither Willa or Isla allowed. I truly couldn't wait to show our new little Simba off. Willa coughed throughout the entire ceremony. I heard it but was not worried. I shrugged it off as one of those "100 day coughs" that kids can get. I trusted that her Body was coughing to get mucus up and out. In addition, three people came up to tell me it sounded like Lil was having a hard time breathing and I assured them that newborns often sound more congested than they are. Which can be true. Being a Mother also requires different levels of worry, and to me at that moment, the girls were okay.

After the ceremony, my Mother mentioned that she was concerned about Willa's cough. I barely listened. I think at this point, my boundaries of trauma had been so blown open, that this felt miniscule in comparison. The next day the girls began to worsen. I had taken Willa to the doctor two times previously about this cough and was assured by her pediatricians that it would pass. It was Sunday night and I decided to take Willa to an emergency pediatric clinic. I also brought Lil along to get checked. As I nonchalantly told the Doctor what was going on with the girls, I saw his face become more and more serious. He said, "I'll be right back." He came back with two nasal swab tests and began to explain that this cough might be RSV. Respiratory Syncytial Virus is a dreaded virus that is dangerous or sometimes fatal for newborns. RSV is sometimes linked to lung issues later on such as allergies and asthma. As we awaited the test results, I began to panic. The tests came back -- they were both positive. The Doctor asked me "What day are you on? When did the symptoms start for the baby?" I replied, day two. He took a big breath and said, "It is going to get worse before it gets better." He gave Lil some steroids to alleviate inflammation, he taught me how to use saline drops in her nose. He reassured me that Willa was okay, but that I needed to watch Lillian very carefully.

I left that place and my heart dropped into my stomach. Like a wartime montage, everything started moving in slow motion. My ears began to ring and I saw Willa talking to me, but I could not hear a thing. Sound started to reemerge as the sound of Lillian's congestion. My eyes felt like they moved forward and locked in a position of watch. My eyes were on guard, ready and waiting for the next bomb to go off. I was immediately back in trauma mode.

Lillian slept a lot the next twelve hours. That next morning, Daryl and I began to notice signs of respiratory distress. Her stomach was pulling in with her inhales. Her nostrils were suctioning closed and her jugular notch was withdrawing. She was actively struggling. She was having a hard time nursing and it became clear that we needed to go to the hospital. We went to a hospital without a children's ER. If you are a caregiver, please listen to me, ALWAYS go to a hospital that has a children's ER -- if you can. I prepared myself for impact and recalled a sense of what might happen. As a young child, I remembered my parents scrambled to get my brother to the hospital for an asthma attack. In those days, you had to go to the hospital for nebulizer treatments. Panic was a part of my childhood, as my brother's Life was often in danger.

When we arrived, I knew they might give her albuterol to see if it would help her breathe. They gave her not one, but two treatments. She was 2 months old. In my opinion that was way too much medication. Her oxygen levels barely improved, but they sent us home anyway. Within two hours of arriving home from the hospital, Lillian began to nose dive. Her breath was still labored and now the number of breaths she was taking a minute was almost double the normal rate. Daryl and I were in shock. I had never had a child go to the hospital and then get worse. I asked Daryl, what should we do and his facial expression of complete terror was the answer. Her Life was in danger and we both knew it.

The drive to the hospital was beyond frightening. I was not sure that she would make it. She was crying, causing her breath to become more erratic. I stopped the car to try and breastfeed her. I was crying and trying so hard to just help her calm down. There was a moment that I froze. I got her to calm down for a moment and didn't know whether to stay there or finish the drive to the hospital. I contemplated driving the rest of the way with her on my breast. I imagined us getting into a car crash and the airbag killing her. I put her back in her car seat and she started crying again. I arrived at the children's ER and we were seen immediately.

Her oxygen was at 90%
Her heartbeats/min were 180
Her breaths/min were 50-60

She was 2 months old and struggling for her Life. They fished for her veins and four attempts later they got an IV in. They hooked her up to an oxygen machine and she began to calm down. Her oxygen levels improved. In less than an hour, we were moved up to the pediatric floor and situated in our own room. These beautiful nurses came in and like angels, set Lil up in her new bed. They dressed her and propped up her little butt with a towel setup, so that she could rest in an inclined position. I will always be grateful for their kindness. One of the nurses went down to the NICU and brought Lillian an ocean themed light and lullaby machine. They told me that she would be here for a few days. I was still nervous and on edge, but Lil looked so calm now. She was sleeping and still working really hard to breathe, but she wasn't fighting it. She looked like she had retreated into a trance. I sat beside her bed, which looked like a tiny prison and just held her hand and whispered to her, Mama is here, I love you. I watched that little ocean go back and forth as I waited and sobbed.

In the middle of the night, the Doctor came in to do her rounds. Lil had started to make these heavy sighs, which almost sounded like sighs of relief. They were little moans. I hadn't thought anything of it, but the Doctor's face went serious. She left the room and when she returned she said, "Mama, we are going to move Lillian down to the PICU. Those sounds she is making are signs of fatigue. She needs more help. We want to make sure she gets it." As they rolled her down to the intensive care unit, my brain started to spiral. Lillian was moved from ER to the Peds Floor to the PICU, there is no other step to go. I just remember tubes everywhere. I remember five people working with her at once. I was in the back row just watching this unfold. It was all moving so fast, that I could not even fathom what this all meant. When the commotion subsided, it was just her and I again. She was still in a trance, pulled deep inside. My eyes were still on guard. I watched her machines like a hawk, monitoring her breath rate, heart rate and oxygen levels every minute of both day and night. I can still hear the beeping machines today.

I could not breastfeed her, so I pumped my milk every two hours to make sure I kept my production up for when we went home. I prayed with every cell of being that we would go home together. The next day they inserted a feeding tube. They asked me to leave while they did this. It took not one, but two tries to succeed. I have regretted leaving the room every day of my Life since. Lil opened her eyes for small periods of time. She would look at me, but she felt very far away. That night, in the room next to us, I listened as a small baby died. I saw her Mother. My heart broke into a million pieces for her. I curled into a ball and wept for her. Life is not fair.

For this week, it was just me and Lil most of the time. Daryl had to be home with the other girls. Daryl would come when he could, of course. We were both beyond frightened. But for the most part, it was just Lil and me. I watched guard and begged her to fight for her Life, and she just quietly endured. She was a different person than her two sisters. Her two sisters were blatant fighters. Willa screeched and burned away every cold in three days. Isla had a steady attack, but usually continued playing through whatever was going on. Lil retreated and that terrified me. It felt like she was not sure if she wanted to be here. My imagination took me to some very dark places that week, so I tried to love her the hardest I could, knowing that nothing was promised. Embodied Life is here and then it isn't. I told her in a hundred ways why Life here is valuable and why I needed her to stay.

By day six, Lillian was on the mend. She started cooing up a storm with the nurses. I began to allow some hope. A day before she came home, we were given the go ahead to breastfeed. I maneuvered her many tubes and my breast and helped her latch. To feel her connected to me was one of the greatest gifts I have ever received. On day seven, she had all her tubes removed and she had to show that she could breathe on her own. Her oxygen levels were still low, but her heart rate and breath rate were much better. We were cleared to go home.

I hadn't seen Isla and Willa in a week because children are not allowed in the PICU and I refused to leave Lillian's side. I hadn't showered and slept maybe three hours a night. When we came home, I watched her breathe every night for the next week until she was fully back to herself. I went out and bought an ocean themed light and lullaby machine. It was more for me than for her.

That week in the PICU changed me. The confidence I felt in the earlier months was now replaced by the title, "Mother-who's-baby-almost-died-because-she-was-too-confident." I was disgusted by my arrogance. I questioned everything about myself. I cleaned obsessively and quarantined every sick person to their room in order to protect Lillian. I could not let her get that sick again.

Lillian continued to throw me wrenches. She had her first ear infection and I was excited. It was not a virus, bacterial infections can be treated! Nope. Lillian broke out in a diffuse rash and was allergic to two antibiotics. I had to be more careful now. I had to look out for viruses and bacterial infections. She developed eczema and we had to invest in seven hundred creams to help her. That summer, we took her to a lake. She loved it! Two days later, she developed staph infection on her legs. She had blisters that were opening and spreading down her legs. We had to clean and surgically bandage her wounds for almost three weeks until it cleared. At two years old, she ate a lego piece. Willa had shoved a lego bow up her nose, but Lil had to eat the lego. Lil also stuck a pea up her nose but I was trained on the art of getting-shit-outta-your-kid's-nose, so I had that pea out in less than 30 seconds.

Lillian still also has croup with almost every respiratory virus. We have had a few trips to the hospital because the inflammation in her throat is intense. She flares up when she is sick. I would be lying if I didn't say that I blame myself. I was under incredible stress during her pregnancy and that comes with a cost. I am so sorry my sweet baby girl. I will be forever sorry.

All of that said, over time, I regained some confidence. Lillian was talking like crazy. She held her own with her sisters. I thought, maybe, we had built up her immunity, so, she began preschool. In just three months of preschool, she was sick almost every other week. After a while, I noticed that Lil began to retreat again. Lil's chipper attitude turned moody. She had multiple ear infections and could not produce a fever. Her sleep was terrible; her congestion was endless. My sleep was deeply affected by this time. I resumed guard. I took pulse/oxygen readings while she was asleep. Counted her breaths/min and took old school heart rate readings because I didn't trust the pulse/oxygen machine. My anxiety quadrupled. I had started to feel very run down, but as a Mother, I didn't have much choice but to keep going. I didn't miss a day of work. I just kept going.

I decided to take her out of preschool the same week that a child in her classroom tested positive for RSV. Lillian had tubes put in her ears and I nursed her back to health. I threw her a beautiful 3rd birthday party and then it all came to a full stop.

In the work of Motherhood, I became lost again. When put all together, this was a 5+ year stretch of trauma, unprocessed trauma. Trauma, in my mind, is a state of overwhelm. Think of a muscle strain. We can strain a muscle because the load of what we are lifting outweighs the strength we have. It can happen in an instant and then it takes time to heal. Trauma in Life has similar conceptual underpinnings. We may try to engage something that is way more complex than what we have energy or resources for. Life may also spontaneously sideswipe us and in a moment we are traumatized. Life can happen so quickly, and as it keeps moving forward, you are dragged under in its momentum -- unable to understand the weight of the impact, unable to process the hurt.

When I was a kid at the Jersey Shore, my Dad taught me how to dive through the waves. As the tide would shift and the waves would increase, I would put my rash shirt on and go in. Each wave looked like a disaster waiting to happen, but I would wait until the very moment before it crashed on me and dive right through the wall of water, as if I was jumping into a parallel Universe. I'd keep my eyes towards the waves and never turn my back on the ocean. It was exhilarating -- but sometimes, I was not fast enough. Sometimes, my timing was off by a millisecond and as I dove into the wave, I didn't slip on through to the otherside, instead the wave's momentum would pull me with it. It felt as if the wave could grab my whole Body, pick it up and smash it down. The pressure of the water would hold me under and I would fight to get to the surface only to face another wave. Without any air or readiness, the next wave would repeat the work of the last. Wave by wave until by some small seeming gift of Grace, the burrage of the waves would cease so that I could get out of the water. This is what these five years felt like.

One trauma has an impact. Endured, sustained trauma is a whole other thing. To understand trauma we must unEarth the truth of our stories. We must go back to the wounds and listen to them. This work is worth the uncomfortable feelings.

For me, I had lived through a period of sustained trauma. I had promised myself that one day, when I was safe, I would come back to process. But my

Body could not wait any longer. A day after Lil's 3rd birthday, I had one of the worst migraines of my Life. I usually have an aura associated with my migraines. I also see this little pixelated snake in my right eye. This time I had two snakes that formed an infinity sign. The pain was intense. The snakes disappeared and as the throbbing in my head increased, I decided to drive myself to the hospital.

That was my first hospital trip of what would be five trips in two months. During each trip, I felt like I was on the brink of a stroke and might die. I was feeling a lot of pain and my anxiety increased exponentially in response to this uptick of symptoms. They were seemingly coming out of nowhere. Everyday I was stopped dead in my tracks, forced to my bed to wait until my whole Body processed each migraine. I desperately tried to figure out what could be causing these attacks. Each hospital visit felt useless. The doctors looked at me like I had six heads. I felt disbelieved each and every time. They would test my heart and blood pressure and then send me home. I would be sent home with diagnoses of hyperventilation syndrome, general anxiety/panic attacks, migraine. They would tell me to follow up with my neurologist. The problem was that I had no real relationship with a neurologist --I had only had migraines infrequently and usually they were associated with a hormonal imbalance. I found a neurologist and he makes me squeeze his fingers and follow his finger back and forth. After a few more basic neurological tests, he tells me that I am fine and puts me on a new medication. I begged him for an MRI of my brain. He responded, "Stay away from doctors, they'll make you sick." He winked and left the room.

The medication created new symptoms of dopiness and a general sense of cloudiness. I kept taking it, because I wanted to feel better. I needed to get back to work and my family. I worked with my General Physician to problem solve my situation. They took many vials of blood and tested me for everything under the sun. All the tests came back negative, except for one. My doctor said to me that I tested positive for bartonella. Bartonella is cat scratch disease, and you can get it from cats or mosquitoes. It can create neurological issues and general disarray in the Body, similar to Lyme disease. I was happy to have a diagnosis. I thought this was it! I had something to treat and I would get better soon. The doctor put me on some homeopathic herbs first, which made things worse, so she then put me on antibiotics. I hate medication and now I was taking two. I didn't feel better, in fact, things worsened. My gums began to blister and I developed vertigo. At this point the migraines were still happening almost everyday. The doctor suggested that I go to an infectious disease doctor and a rheumatologist. I went to both and more vials of blood were drawn. All of the tests came out negative, including bartonella. The infectious disease doctor informed me that my GP was an idiot and that she had read the report incorrectly, so for twenty days, I had taken antibiotics unnecessarily.

I was losing hope. I was spiralling downward. There were days that my brain felt so dissonant that the room looked like it was shaking. I would sink into the depths of myself, unsure if I could resurface. One image that would recur was of me, sinking to the bottom of the sea. I wasn't drowning, I was just falling deeper and deeper. I would eventually reach the bottom. It was quiet and dark there. It felt safe there, just me and this vast Body of water. In my despair, I would ask this Body of energy around me questions and it would answer me:

Am I okay?

                          Of course, you are.

Am I going to die?

                                      No.

Is it this worst-case scenario?

                                      No.

Are you sure?

                                     Yes.

Am I safe?

                             Yes, always.

I just kept asking questions until I felt better. In
time, I would come to understand that this Body of
water was my Body.

In the meantime, I felt like no one really cared for
me and my health. The western medical system is
so specialized that it forces the patient to manage
their whole case, alone. I was trying to put the
pieces together from all of these doctors and feeling
incredibly discouraged. So with great resolve, I
sought out a new neurologist. I was determined to
have an MRI. The hospital had taken a CT scan and
it was, of course, all clear. I was convinced that all
of these doctors were missing something. How
could I experience all of this pain with no structural

cause? That didn't make sense to me. Yet. The ironic part of my story was that I had spent the past two years taking continuing education programs studying pain and the nervous system. I already had the understanding of why I was in so much pain, but I was too close to see it. I met with the new neurologist and he was the first doctor that seemed at all interested in helping me get better. The first question that he asked me was if I had trouble sleeping. Of course, I had just spent the past three months taking care of Lil all hours of the day. I had lived in hypervigilance mode for almost 5+ years to boot. Next, he asked me if I meditated or knew some breathing techniques. I giggled in annoyance to myself. I am a Yoga Teacher and knew all of these techniques. I had shrugged them off. Last, he asked me if I had trauma in my past. I nodded yes and felt tears well up in my eyes. I started to soften to the truth I already knew. These migraines were a physiological expression of my unprocessed trauma. He recommended EMDR[1] therapy and sent me for an MRI. The MRI was clear. I had no issues in my tissues.

Pain is a fascinating subject. It feels like the worst experience in the world. Pain can make us all feel like our Bodies are betraying us. In actuality, pain is your friend. A physiological expression that is always acting out of protection. However, this protection can be overprotective and even that response is caused. Pain is complex. It is biological, psychological and sociological. Each of us has developed unique pain expressions curated over the span of our entire lives. Pain is biological -- falling down and scraping your knee. This acute trauma creates tissue damage and the Body responds biochemically to attend to the new wound. Pain is psychological -- we all learn how to emotionally attend to the wound. Think about when you were young and you fell down, what was the response you heard the most? "You're fine, get up." Or, "Oh my goodness, oh no, this is bad." Through these responses, we learn how to respond to pain. We may learn to listen, panic, get angry, cry or ignore it. Pain is sociological -- do you have the financial resources to investigate pain? Can you take off of work to heal? Are you a caregiver and overrun with tasks and the demands of your family? I have just described the Biopsychosocial model of Pain[2] (BPS), which has been gaining steam for the past 20+ years. It is a different orientation than the dominant biomedical model of pain. The biomedical model prioritizes purely biological factors and excludes psychological, environmental and social influences. The biomedical model works really well for big pharmaceutical companies.

However, for folks like me and everyone else, the BPS model includes the fuller story of how pain develops. The biomedical model is the reason we have an opioid crisis on our hands. Oh you have pain? There is a pill for that. The danger of the biomedical model discounts a person's psychological and social experience. It also underestimates the power of the nervous system and the stunning and still yet to be understood nuances of the Body.

Pain is created by our nervous system. In our Bodies, we have nociceptors,[3] which are sensory receptors that detect danger. When they detect danger they relay that information to the central nervous system for further processing. Some things are reflexively taken care of from the spinal cord, other stimulus needs further analysis and is processed in the brain. The important thing to understand is that even though these nociceptors can detect danger, they cannot express pain. Pain comes from the brain. The nervous system expresses pain as a protective mechanism to keep you alive. Because there are not clearly delineated pain expressors, each person's Body expresses pain differently. You may have IBS, panic attacks, knee pain, back pain, or migraines. Pain expression is your Body communicating to you to pay attention.

Furthermore, pain can be trained. We are what we do the most. For example, if you pulled your back out in Yoga class in a forward fold, your Body remembers that. It tags it. You may have had some back pain, perhaps even a herniated disc. Instead of listening to the aches and pains, you tried Yoga class and one forward fold later you can't stand up. Let's just say that it takes weeks to feel better. In response to the pain, you begin to guard your back. You worry each time you need to bend down and pick something up. Every time you see an image of a Yoga class, you recall what happened and feel pain. In order to avoid having another back incident you limit working out, you sit more and your back pain increases. You start to hate everyone who loves Yoga and blame Yoga class for your pain. Your back pain is now an everyday issue and you resign to the idea that you are broken, for good. Every sentence I just wrote in this hypothetical narrative is a *neurotag*.[4] Your brain makes markers to remember pain. Why? For your survival. Is it the most effective and conscious process? No. Can we engage with our pain? Yes. Can it get better? Yes.

When we have experienced pain chronically, the neurotags are vast and join together to make strong neuro signatures or circuits. The more time in that loop, the deeper the grooves in the brain, the more reactive the circuits become. Pain can be a very effective brain pathway. In some situations pain is a response to an acute injury. Here the biomedical model might fare well. But chronic injury, trauma, and neural pathway pain are different beasts. Chronic pain is grooved in our biology and psychology fed by sociological and environmental pressures. Consistent pain requires a lot of investigation into past events and present triggers. It requires time. Time is void in our present healthcare system. Instead, opioids are the current answer.

What became crystal clear to me, was that my pain was an overactive response of my nervous system caused by years of sustained trauma and hypervigilance, so I settled into the journey of understanding my pain. I went on an inner quest to listen to my migraines. The etymology of the word quest is *to ask*, so I began to ask my Body what was wrong? I began a deep dialogue of why I was hurting. I started EMDR therapy to actively process my past events. EMDR therapy continues to teach me how to access my memory and heal. I had to go back to the moments that caused fear and allow the room to feel the sadness, hurt, and betrayal. I had to trust my pain to find my healing.

Fun fact: In advanced stage scurvy, when the Body is at a dangerous deficit of vitamin c, every wound that person has ever had begins to reopen.[5] That paper cut in the fourth grade is still in there. This truth confirms two things:

One, the Body remembers.

Two, it is constantly doing the work of healing you.

The Body remembers everything, even when we forget that. We can think that we have forgotten the hardships of our Life, that the past stays in the past. In reality, the past lives with us, in the fabric of our being, and when we allow it space in the context of our Life, pain quiets down.

Pain is always protective and preempted by a loss of safety first. Pain keeps you out of danger and calls you to attend and listen inward. Pain is not your enemy, it is evidence of your aliveness. When we can soften into our pain, we walk the Mobiüs strip[6] straight into the other side. The other side of continuous healing and affirmation of Life. We are fullness in form. Our Bodies hold us even when we feel the worst, all the while beckoning us to enjoy the ride.

I continue the work it takes to heal and the migraines have decreased. I now have only 3-5 a month and they seem to still be on the decline. I trust in time, they will resolve almost completely. The severity of the migraines is a fraction of the pain I was experiencing. I can often even breathe my way out of a migraine. How? Because my brain tissues are fine. My pain is latent unprocessed memory. Like a small child, there are parts of my experience that I couldn't fathom as possible, nor did I have the time to feel what I was feeling or understand the experience as it happened at the time. As I uncover these parts, as they are heard and felt, they easily fade into the background. They stop howling at me, begging me to listen to them. Like the Wild Woman.

This is the dialogue of one of my more recent therapy sessions:

Therapist: Can you ask the Wild Woman what she wants to say? Is there something she wants you to know?

Me: Sure.
She is howling.
She is compelling, and I want to listen, but I am scared I will become lost in her fury. I am afraid she will show me more trauma hidden.

{Silence}

Me: Okay, I'll ask her.

{ I start tapping[7]. I turn towards her rage. In a breath, this blood-smeared goddess quieted, like Kali in rage suddenly interrupted by a crying baby. She begins to tell me that she just needed me to listen.}

Wild Woman: How come you won't listen? I had to ask your grandmother (who has passed) to nudge you to listen to that intuitive (who you didn't believe) to come back to your Body. I tried to get you to meditate, to stop. But you wouldn't stop. So I stopped you.

Me: That was you? All those Migraines?

Wild Woman: Yes. I was trying to hold you. I am your Body. You can rest in me.

{As she says these words, it feels like falling backward with soft negative pressure. I am sucked backward, out of the intense forward gaze of my eyes. In a breath, I feel supported}

Wild Woman: You are Self-sustaining. You have always been. There is nothing you need to do to be nourished. Only stop and rest sometimes. I will do the work for you.

Me: Can I trust the world?

Wild Woman: Yes and No. You must still hold protection. It all comes back to the same energy though, so you can also release into it.

Me: Who are you?

Wild Woman: Your parasympathetic nervous system. Santhana Lakshmi[8]. I am you, as you recognize yourself on that beach, that summer, with Lil in your belly and Isla and Willa by your side. I am you, as you recognize yourself at that temple with the small Ganesha, where the ground felt like it was feeding you. I am you when you recognize yourself. That feeling of deep security, that visceral sense of safety from you, as you.

{I know her. I stop tapping}

_____

Do not be afraid of your pain.

Move gently towards it. Your healing and your fullness are all there waiting for you.

5: Resolute

Never have I ever...this much
Cooked
Cleaned
Gone on so many walks
Grieved
Rode bikes with my children
Taken so much Yoga
Celebrated the most straightforward things
Connected so purposefully with my loved ones
Dreamed
Been this disillusioned
Wondered about where we go next
Marveled at how cool the Earth is
Hugged my parents' legs so they can feel my love
Created date night dinner with my husband in the
basement
Smelled the air as if it would disappear
Thanked my lungs for every breath
Been so disappointed in people
Had to hold light and protection for so many
passing
Felt gratitude for those who are holding up the rest
of us
Laughed and cried with my daughters
Seen my children work it through with each other

Thought about my whiteness
Realized all the ways I have unconsciously
participated in systemic racism
Been so embarrassed to be an American
Received the depth of brutality and violence
committed against BIPOC
and LGBTQIA+ community
Felt extreme rage for the inequity of our country
Cried so hard, screaming at my phone, "Get off of
his neck"
Opened my mouth this much
Written
Held my partnership so tight
Been so aware of how hurtful my words can be
Embraced my own ignorance, internalized privilege
and biases
Celebrated our ability to feel
Held such steadfastness
Listened to learn and acknowledge my failures
Been so scared of white fragility, empowered by
power and prejudice
Been so disgusted by the police and those who
continue to stick up for them
Watched videos of protesters being beaten and
gassed and killed
Seen my babies process a pandemic through their
physiology

Let go of hope, because it is the delusion of the
colonizer
Seen guinea pigs fight for dominance
Trusted my sense of Self
Given back value to my emotional and wild Self
Understood the level of trauma bred by our society
Been more resolved to change the fucking world
Realized that I am on a Mobius strip
Until now.

• • •

Every year I read and discuss the Bhagavad Gita[1]
with my Yoga teacher trainees, and every year,
based on where I am in my Life, a new passage or
idea feels illuminated. This year, we happen to be
reading the Gita through a Global Pandemic and a
renewed awakening for Social Justice. The
takeaways have never felt more relevant. In chapter
sixteen of the Gita, Krishna (who is God) explains to
Arjuna (I am paraphrasing, but it goes a little
something like this):

- Virtue is not something that you acquire.
  Virtue comes naturally when the yogin
  understands their place in the Eternal and in
  the materiality of the world. Furthermore,

when the yogin has cultivated a deep sense of their own Body, mind, and heart, they will act in inherently virtuous ways.

- Evil is not our nature. Evil is an expression of one's refusal to engage in anything greater than oneself. The path of evil is a path of isolation to the whole.

At the heart of these great teachings is an essential idea. That we are *never-not* yoked to the fullness of the Universe, only the idea/delusion exists that we are separate and must find our way back. The yogin is one who can see through the illusion of duality as they move through the differentiated world. And because they understand reality as non-dual, they act in the embodied world with the consciousness of the infinite. When one knows themself as an expression of Life, one acts to uphold Life itself. That is the epitome of virtue.

It has taken me time to place my heart in this understanding -- that no matter what, I am hitched to the essence of Life itself; that I am an expression of the Multiverse. I have the words *You are the secret the universe is telling*[2] tattooed on my right forearm, and I still had a hard time believing it. My trained cognitive brain is strong. I have resisted releasing into the felt sense of safety deep within my being because of my pragmatic and proof-loving ways. I have always asked for evidence to accept that something is true. Or to be more exact, I have learned that I need scientific proof of something for it to be true. In my ongoing decolonizing work and in unpacking my whiteness, I have come to understand that so much of my characteristic mannerisms are internalized learnings of patriarchy and white supremacy.

Things like:
-Rugged self-reliance
-Highly valued independence and autonomy
-Orientation around action
-Must always do something attitude
-Politeness, even when emotions say otherwise
-Hard work is the key to success
-Emphasis on scientific method
-Priority to objective, rational linear thinking
-Value of Self-based on job success
-Winner-loser dichotomy[3]

If I strip away my indoctrinated beliefs, an interesting thing starts to happen. I find myself in this curious space of wonder. Without those assumptions, what do I feel now? What is the essence of my being before I learned all this culture? And now that I see all of these cultured ideas, how will that change the way I act in the world? Yoga, as I see it, is a practice of conscious relationship. I see my place in the differentiated and embodied world, and I see the paradoxical illusion of separation from the Universe. By understanding my own mortal, conditioned reality, I can receive my participation in the immortal movement of Life. Being yoked is a state of knowing the complexity of being in the world and its terms AND being in the greater context, simultaneously. Like water through a sieve or blood as it filters through an organ, I move through the world, and the world moves through me. I am aware and yet transparent, steadfast in an attuned state of feeling.

When I went to India, one of my favorite rituals to experience was with the Goddess Kali.[4] At one part in the ritual, they bathed her in sesame oil and dark red kumkum powder. She was wearing a white dress, and as the oil and kumkum saturated her dress, she looked like she was bleeding. To top it all off a cockroach climbed across her face. That experience resonated in my heart. That experience could not only be expressed in scientific terms. It was not *just* cognitive -- it was also *visceral*. I felt her blood as my blood. I felt her primal raging Self as the ferocity of my being. I was the resilient cockroach. Life is powerful, and I am Life. I am not suggesting that cognition is the enemy. It is out of balance. Awareness has been given the title of "better" over the visceral sense of our aliveness. Because our primal selves are not so easily quantified or proved, they are often dismissed in patriarchal societies. To be explicit: In our society.

I have been urged to remember to include the voices of the Feminine energy of Life. When only one voice acts in isolation and disconnects from the whole, this is evil -- We must remember Mother Earth in connection to Father Sky. The feminine, masculine, and non-binary are within all of us. Failure is a form of learning. Rest is an action. My Life, your Life, is evidence of success. All of these ideas are here and valuable too.

What plagues the Western ideologies is that they forget we are a part of a whole -- Mother Earth forgotten, us as a part of nature forgotten, Earth as a part of the Multiverse forgotten. Let me say it again: The only fall from Grace, as I see it, is that we forgot we cannot fall from Grace. We cultured ourselves out of nature. We have created a great big lie to blow smoke up our own asses. We have convinced ourselves that we are in control and autonomous. Our independence will eventually be reconciled, even if that means our species' total annihilation by Mother Earth. Walk the Mobiüs strip long enough, and it flips you the other way.

Our society, our world, is in an emergent expression of pain. This current painful expression is urging us to listen and remember. Pain emerges as a response, an alert to bring attention back to the whole, and the participation of each part in the whole. Emergence[5] is a fundamental concept in complex adaptive systems, i.e., Life in general, You. A visual depiction of emergence is seen in the swirling and differentiated patterns of snowflakes. Society is also emergent. Start with humans as individuals, then consider their interactions. From their many relationships, a structure is born. It is born out of the individual overlapping connections. Then the emergent system creates a hierarchical influence back down to the individuals from which it emerged. The emergent structure we find ourselves (our current version of society) affects the whole. However, this emergent structure and pain are still dependent on the underlying parts and their relationships to each other. Emergence offers us a way to consider ourselves. You and I all have a role in the structures that define us. We impress change on the whole.

This era has been marked by tragedy and violence -- a hard price to pay. It has also given way to exposition and voice. Everything that is illuminated now has been here all along, waiting to be uncovered. The word apocalypse means uncovering, and we are indeed in an apocalyptic world. In a cascade of isolation and control based behaviors, we have created a polarized society of greed, dominance, and genocidal behavior. Reduction, linear and centralized structures are what brought us here. I was blown away by the talent in the show *Hamilton,* and as I watched, it was evident that here in the "United" States, we are still playing out the displacement of our trauma from our colonizers. We fought for freedom from our colonizers to turn around and continue the colonizing behaviors of slavery, indigenous genocide and misogyny. Americans have not processed their trauma. We never felt the pain of loss, the deep grief of our afflicted and endured violence. Those wounds have continued to fester,[6] calling for attention.

I would argue this even further back. Back to when we thought of ourselves as animals. Even back to that one cell that ate another cell. Living on Earth has always included a fight for food, space, and dominance. That is a challenging idea to swallow. We may need to review Darwin again. We have forgotten our own mortality and connection to this fight for Life.

This summer, our family adopted guinea pigs, two males, and after about two months, they started to fight for dominance. The bigger one would hump the smaller one. The smaller one would squeal in defense and eventually get himself out from under the bigger guinea pig. My eldest daughter was mortified, one because of the humping, and two, that her guinea pig was aggressive to her sister's guinea pig. We did some research, and apparently, this behavior will continue until one of them submits. We see this in dogs and other animal species. We just don't want to accept that we, humans, are doing the same thing.

As Homosapiens, we now have these big brains that can think big thoughts. We can work together and find solutions for living, sharing resources, and producing respectful relationships with each other and the world. Some are trying to work from this point of view. Others are just fighting for dominance in the cage, holding onto their delusional narrative. Life is complex, and our behaviors have been learned or forced for survival, not conscious thought. DNA has encoded our experiences and passed them down, and that is not a problem to be solved. We just need to add more perspective back in. We can open our eyes, receive our causality, yoke it back to the whole through feeling, through reparations and dare I say it -- through Love.

In Douglas Brooks' book *Poised for Grace*,[7] he writes, "Love is no simple matter. It will require assiduous Yoga and application." To escape Armageddon, it's going to take a massive movement of conscious connection back to the essential energy that birthed us all. Whatever you want to call it is fine by me, but we were created from the Earth and beyond, and she will take us back down to dust. Love requires listening. Love requires remembering our connection. Love requires Yoga, the perspective that we are *never-not* yoked to the fullness of everything else. If you violate others, you violate yourself, you violate Life.

Today as I write this, there have been 207k deaths[8] from Covid-19 in the United States. We are watching innumerable deaths in the name of white supremacy. The *Bhagavad Gita* is still so relevant and powerful today because this narrative's characters stand on the precipice of familial war, relatives killing relatives.[9] This story is our story, alive and well today -- we still don't possess this understanding. This moment in time feels urgent to me. It is calling us all to re-cognize ourselves in relationship to everything else. We need to re-search what we have been continuing with every breath of complacency. If we are doing this right, we are going to have to make new choices. We will lose connections and stand for better ones. I see the fear in so many, afraid of "losing" their way of Life - as if losing their status in white supremacy is a cool status to have in the first place. That line of thinking erases connection to the whole; it erases other expressions of Life. It creates a dangerous hierarchy and this is a demonic path.

Running a community/business has been quite an experience in all of this. Our Yoga studio is our family business and our livelihood. It is also simultaneously a community of people. We have been learning and moving together through Life for the past eighteen years, and I consider it both a business and a community. I love this community as my family. My husband and I have fought for this community with our actual blood, sweat, and tears. With the warnings of the health risks of COVID-19, we were one of the first studios to move our brick and mortar Yoga studio to the cloud.

To help with morale, I began to write an email a day. These emails initially started as logistical communication. Then they began to morph. Embedded in them was a daily journal of Life in these times. I wrote for 100 days straight. In these 100 emails, I thought out loud, I asked questions, and tried to rally the community. You can feel my effort in each email. The first three weeks have an innocent enthusiasm, like, "We got this." "Keep going." The tone then changes in correlation to the number of losses. The spike of the curve hit hard. As I wrote them, I lost my ability to express how I was feeling. I needed just to feel the pain of losing so many loved ones, so suddenly. I started to feel a bit at war with myself. As a well-indoctrinated woman of western thought, I fell back to the default ideology of keep the momentum going -- stay positive. But as a person, and as a part of this community, I wanted just to hold space for the grief and fear.

As time went on, we ran right into our humanity again. Around day 68 of the shelter in place, there was a rise of unrest. People were "done" with COVID even though COVID was not done with them. The itchiness of this time was to be expected. Will-power is a costly endeavor by a human Body. In the case of COVID, we all began to run out of steam. Folks were losing their jobs, running out of money, getting sick, and being forced to live in insular and perhaps abusive situations. Processing this time's mental health crisis will be part of our work in the decades to come. The bottom line became evident. Practicing caution every minute of the day is difficult. Focused, intentional action for primates is short-lived -- it is energetically expensive. Habit, therefore, is cheap.[10]

As I wrote the emails, I tried to affirm how hard this place was/is. I encouraged the community to move, rest, and allow time for emotions and processing. Up to this point, I felt okay in my ability to navigate the business/community/personal/public. That is, until George Floyd's death. As I watched that beloved man murdered by a white man bred by white supremacy, I thought to myself, this is Hell on Earth. As he cried out for his Mama, I felt him as my son. I felt his loss as his Mother.

I have never considered myself an activist, but when you see all beings yoked to the fullness of the Universe, there is no problem taking up activism. Standing up against inequity is not a hard job. It is my Dharma[11] as a conscious being. It is my duty to remember our inherent connection and fight for those being pushed to the margins, discriminated against for false and antiquated ideologies. When I find that hatred in myself, I will also do the work of Dharma in myself. I do not believe in spiritual bypassing[12] the hard realities around us because within those wounds lies our context and healing[13].

As I wrote more daily emails and stood up for Black Lives Matter, I received more and more emails of negative feedback. "This is a business and no place for your opinion." "Racism is an opinion, and it is not my opinion." To which I responded, my business is woven inextricably with my voice, and Racism is not an opinion or belief. Racism is a series of intended structures and practices created to divert power and resources to white people.

I stood up for Defunding the Police and lost more students. One email I received started with the sentence, "Defund my membership." It is sad to see so many opt out of the conversation. I wish I said more to the client who asked to defund their membership. Defunding the police means that more funds go to resources for community services, not to the police's militarization. We must talk this through.

When a child misbehaves, we have been inculcated to dominate that child into submission, "Shut up or else." There is endless research about self-regulation[14] skills that all start from the same place -- we are mammals. When you are over-tired, under-fed, under moved, lacking resources, we act out. We act out because our basic needs are not met. Our country is built on the foundation that only white men are created equal. Everyone else is starved of resources on purpose. And let me be clear, there are hierarchies of discrimination and they overlap. This is called intersectionality[15] and it matters. Those with the greatest intersectionality, feel the most trauma, discrimination, etc and often suffer the most in terms of health. Defund the police, means take away money from an organization that is built on white guys and their fraternity and reinvest in the well being of the whole. Defunding the police is Yoga. It yokes the individuals back into the relationship as a whole. If you are a cop reading this, you should be fighting for the same cause. You want to be good cops -- give up your power and serve the people in a way that actually works to protect and serve. When a cop violates someone for peacefully protesting, he has fallen down a demonic path. Even if as a cop, you do not commit the crimes and still stand in brethren with those who do, I would say you have lost sight of your connection to something greater. Even if these words make you uncomfortable, then I would invite you to sit in that uncomfortability and understand where it is coming from. Follow it all the way back to you are *never-not* connected to everything else and then do better.

In moments like this, when the pain is screaming from the depths of our commingled existence to pull us back to our Mother, Earth, I will fight for that. We all have no idea where we came from or where we are going, but I have agency in the great dramedy that is this Life. I will not stand for cruelty and domination. I have been raped before, and you better believe that I will not stand by as white fragility continues to force itself on everyone. If this is all a dream and we have a choice, then I stand for Dharma. Yoga has taught me to see my agency, to embrace my narrative and pain. It has also reminded me of my connection to everyone else. It has given me ways never to forget that everyone comes from something. We are all caused, whether that is predestined or spontaneous or a mix of both. We are caused and have agency. You have a choice on how you want to participate in Life. As we move through the world, it moves through us.

May we allow this moment to impact us, to remind us of our connection. We are one and the many. If we forget this, we are lost. Even as I write this, I want to make sure that the words I choose do not fuel this familial war. In time, I may be eaten by the other cell -- For this moment I am resolute as I stand for Life. I want us all to celebrate Life in all expressions. I believe in equity and the mechanisms it creates to disperse society's resources in ways that affirm Life.

To close, I have been working on birthing a new Yoga program for children based on the nervous system, the BPS model of Pain, and self-regulation skills. I have had the pleasure of working with ten other brilliant minds.[16] Together we have put a program together in the heart of inclusivity and connection. We have created an affirmation for our children's program to say each and every class. This affirmation brings together what I have learned during this time. It summarizes my approach as a Body in the world, connected to others, empowered with agency.

May this affirmation remind you of your place in it all. May you take up the cause of standing for Life with me.

I come from something
My Life is valuable (and so is yours)
I am multifaceted and everyone else is
multifaceted too
My actions affect change
Everything is allowed
{Repeat until needed}

Abhinavagupta[17] describes an essential equation and Douglas Brooks reiterates it in these terms:

The way the world really is = the way things can be = the way we should act.

The radiance of the world is calling us to remember. The continuity of Life is urging us to include each other's differences as a reflection of our own fullness. Joy is a practice of recognition of what is already there. May we renew the brilliance of the *Bhagavad Gita* and find ourselves in this same pressing moment. Just as Krishna ends the *Gita* with the beautiful line, "Do as you wish," may we all consider how we want to participate in the world and what we uphold. The fight for Life or the fight for dominance?

Epilogue:

At the end of the book *Illusions* by Richard Bach, he states:

All of this could be wrong.

When I read that line for the first time, it caught me off guard. It made me think about why he wrote it in the first place. I questioned its placement. Even though it was the last line of the book, it propelled me forward into deeper thinking. Like, when you forget the last step at the bottom of the staircase and your momentum hurls you forward.

As I finished this book of memories and stories, I wanted to include my version of, "All of this could be wrong." I want to make sure that this small book stays alive. I do not wish to have these words cemented in posterity. Memory changes, stories continue to unfold and make sense in new ways. As I grow up and into more of my Life, I want to make sure that I can come back and revisit these words. I want to come back and see my mistakes embedded in the words. I like the task of rewriting and repairing those mistakes and breathing new perspectives into what is already there.

I envision this collection of narrative as a recursive journey. This is why I self-published, so that I can change my mind at any point. So that writing this truly was an expression of my generative, receptive and continuous Self. The power of the feminine energy of Life is that she receives, generates, and continues. This work will endure. This work is from my understanding of the world now. This work will continue because I will continue.

If you have made it this far and are reading these words right now -- thank you.

Before we leave each other, let's just come back to the P A U S E.

Take a comfortable seat once again.

Make sure you have support around you so that your Body can relax into the structures beneath and beside you.

Come sit with yourself, like a trusted friend.

Move towards the movement of your own breath. Feel its welcome.

Let your cells relax.
Invite your breath to expand.

Follow it, in its intrinsic pulsation.
Up and down.
Inhale to exhale.

Follow this space.
Follow the feeling within your being.
Come on down to the physical sensations.

Follow it far enough that you F E E L your
connection to everything else.

What do you notice?

Acknowledgments:

To my collective of Grandmothers -- I hear you dear ones and thank you for your guiding wisdom from beyond. Thank you for your whispers of the girls' names, the deep lines of reassurance and the all around wonder of Life as it is. Thank you for all the images you plant in my mind or the memories you have formed in my being. I am listening.

Mom & Dad -- You are golden spirits of love and support. I am so grateful to you. I know that I come from Love and, therefore can continue in Love and for Love. Thank you for holding me throughout my Life.

Evan, my brother -- You have seen me through all my iterations. Thank you for calling me your SiSTAR and writing funny birthday cards that always make me cry. One day I hope we live close and don't have to repeat Fievel every night. Love you.

Vishali -- Thank you for sharing your wisdom. This book is proof of your excellence as a Teacher. I am assimilating how I am using Yoga, all of which I learned from you. It will not compare to your virtuosity. Thank you for your generosity. Thank you for believing in me and bestowing within me such embedded processes of Life.

Alison -- Without you, this book would not be here. I would have given up on the value of my words a long time ago. Thank you for seeing this through with me. Thank you also for holding onto the magic of Life with me. I am so grateful and inspired by your poetry, art, and creative wisdom. Now we must birth your book, next.

The Yoga Mechanics community -- I learned most of what I have written down here from the work we have done together. Thank you for trusting me with your stories and letting me journey along with you.

Lastly --This book is also dedicated to anyone who felt something in their Body and trusted it, beyond the many who doubted them. What you know to be true in your Body is important.

Endnotes:

Cover

I am purposefully capitalizing this word through this book. I will also capitalize other words like Life, Mother, Motherhood, Father and others. I understand that they are common nouns. I am choosing to acknowledge these words and their weight and complexity.

Epigraph

Thank you Toni Morrison. I am forever changed by your brilliance. Morrison, Toni. *Beloved*: A Novel. New York: Knopf, 1987. Print.

Introduction

1 - *Why is synaptic pruning important for the developing brain?* in SA Mind 28, 3, 75 (May 2017) doi:10.1038/scientificamericanmind0517-75
I don't necessarily love this article for all info about synaptic pruning but the first line is perfectly stated. For more information about synaptic pruning, see here:
https://en.wikipedia.org/wiki/Synaptic_pruning

2 - Vishali Varga is a renowned Yoga Teacher and LCSW. She is my mentor and brilliant beyond words. She is my most influential teacher. She can be found at www.wisdomwithintherapy.com.

3 - The Yoga Studio is called Yoga Mechanics, located in Montclair, NJ. www.yogamechanics.com

1: Learning through the lens of the Body

1 - *Illusions* by Richard Bach is an engaging story about a Messiah turned mechanic, Donald Shimoda and, his conversations with a pilot, Richard. The red bi-plane reminds me of my connection to my Dad and the blue feather represents my Mother. I also chose these two tattoos because the images cull up ideas of will and agency that I loved and wanted to remember. Bach, Richard, *Illusions: The Adventures of a Reluctant Messiah*. New York: Dell/E. Friede, 19811977

2 - More on embryonic development and stem cells:
https://en.wikipedia.org/wiki/Embryonic_development
https://en.wikipedia.org/wiki/Embryonic_stem_cell

3 - Domain (Biology) -
https://en.wikipedia.org/wiki/Domain_(biology)

4 - Quote from Owen Flanagan (1992)

5 - Me Generation -
https://en.wikipedia.org/wiki/Me_generation

6 - Nancy Bannon - https://www.nancybannon.com/bio

7 - Laban/Bartenieff Movement Studies -
https://labaninstitute.org

8 - The Yoga studio was called Yoga Mandali Montclair, founded by Vishali Varga in Montclair, NJ. She eventually renamed the studio Yoga Montclair. This studio was an Anusara Yoga studio and the foundation of my Yoga journey.

9 - Douglas Brooks has been an extremely important teacher in my Life. He, alongside Vishali Varga, has been my philosophy teacher throughout my Yoga career. He is an

invaluable resource and guide. He can be found at https://rajanaka.com.

10 - *The Bhagavad Gita in the Mahabharata* by J. A. B. Van Buitenen. Chicago: University of Chicago Press, 1981

11 - "Dr. Gopala Aiyar Sundaramoorthy (b.1936-d.1994) Affectionately known as "Appa," the Tamil word for "Father," Dr. Douglas Brooks became Appa's student in 1977, lived in his home for many years, and continued studies with him until Appa's death in 1994. Appa was a scholar, community leader, and activist, and a family man, he was Chair of the Department of Sanskrit at Madurai-Kamaraj University in Madurai, Tamil Nadu, India, and was pivotal in guiding Dr. Brooks' along his own academic and spiritual path." sourced from https://rajanaka.com.

12 - Thank you Vishali for teaching me these ideas.

13 - Anusara Yoga - Anusara moved forward as an organization and the strong and wonderful teachers committed to the method reclaimed it. They took the beauty of the technique and birthed it anew. They took a complicated situation and transmuted it. Anusara taught me so much of what I know, and I give it great credit always. Although I did not move forward with the organization, I am lucky to have secure connections with this community still. https://www.anusaraYoga.com

14 - John Friend - https://en.wikipedia.org/wiki/John_Friend_(yogi)

2: Reclaim Movement

1 - If you haven't watched the National Geographic Series called *One Strange Rock*, you must.

2 - For further information on our species' evolution, I recommend reading *Sapiens* by Yuval Noah Harari.

3 - Read *The Story of the Human Body: Evolution, Health, and Disease* by Daniel Lieberman and *Born to Run: A Hidden Tribe, Superathletes, and the Greatest Race the World Has Never Seen* by Christopher McDougall

4 - *Move Your DNA* by Katy Bowman is one of the most influential books in my career as a movement professional. I highly encourage you to purchase and read this book. The information in this book will transform the way you see the world.

5 - *Moana* is a 2016 American 3D computer-animated musical adventure film produced by Walt Disney Animation Studios and released by Walt Disney Pictures. I don't always like Disney, but this one is worth the watch.

6 - More on evolutionary mismatch: https://en.wikipedia.org/wiki/Evolutionary_mismatch

3: *Holding Life*

1 - Rev. Karma Cloud is a powerful creator, artist, Mother, guide. You can find her at https://www.sowisdom.com.

2 - More on Maternal, Fetal and Infant Mortality Rates due to structural racism: https://www.ncbi.nlm.nih.gov/pmc/articles/PMC5915910/ I also recommend learning from Shafia Monroe; she is a force of truth and has a rich commitment to public health. You can find her at:

https://shafiamonroe.com/keynote-motivational-speaking/birt
h-justice-movement/

3 - Thank you, Evan Harder.

4: Emergence

1 - EMDR stands for Eye Movement Desensitization and
Reprocessing. This type of therapy has proven to be extremely
useful in my healing story and ongoing mental health. Read
more about it here:
https://en.wikipedia.org/wiki/Eye_movement_desensitization_
and_reprocessing

2 - BPS model of pain. BPS stands for the Biopsychosocial
model of pain. This model contrasts the Biomedical model of
pain. Learn more about these two models here:
- Biomedical model -
  https://en.wikipedia.org/wiki/Biomedical_model
- Biopsychosocial model -
  https://en.wikipedia.org/wiki/Biopsychosocial_model
- I learned about the BPS model in my continuing
  education process with these organizations:
  - www.rocktape.com
  - https://themovementmaestro.com/maestro-co
    urses/
  - https://www.noigroup.com

3 - Our feeling Body has many Mechanoreceptors; these
receptors sense all kinds of stimuli and relay that information
to the Central Nervous System. Read more here:
https://en.wikipedia.org/wiki/Mechanoreceptor

Nociceptors are danger detecting receptors. They, however, cannot produce pain. They detect noxious stimuli and relay that information to the CNS. Read more here: https://en.wikipedia.org/wiki/Nociceptor

4 - For more information on Neurotags and their role in chronic pain. Read *Explain Pain or Explain Supercharged* by G. Lorimer Moseley and David S. Butler.

Also see Ronald Melzack here: https://en.wikipedia.org/wiki/Ronald_Melzack.

5 - The quote below continues to astound me. The understanding of how our collagen is continuously repaired is magnificent to me. Manaugh seems to take this quote and reduce it down to the Body's inability to heal. I think it is even cooler than that. What I hear in this quote is that the Body remembers its wounds and continuously repairs them. Holding Life together is an ongoing process. Thank you, Jonathan Ballone, for sharing this with me. Here is the quote as it was shared with me:

Infinite Exchange
by Geoff Manaugh
1. In a 2011 paper on the medical efforts of scurvy, author Jason C. Anthony offers a remarkable detail about human Bodies and the long-term presence of wounds. "Without vitamin C," Anthony writes, "we cannot produce collagen, an essential component of bones, cartilage, tendons, and other connective tissues. Collagen binds our wounds, but that binding is replaced continually throughout our lives. Thus in advanced scurvy" - reached when the Body has gone too long

without vitamin C - "old wounds long thought healed will magically, painfully reappear."

In a sense, there is no such thing as healing. From paper cuts to surgical scars, our Bodies are catalogs of wounds: imperfectly locked doors quietly.

6 - Vishali has long used this image of the Mobius strip. Vish, you are the queen of metaphor/ analogy. If you don't know what a Mobius strip is, see here:
https://en.wikipedia.org/wiki/Möbius_strip

7 - Tapping Therapy and Thought Field Therapy, created by Dr. Roger Callahan.

8 - Santhana Lakshmi is an iteration of the Hindu Goddess Lakshmi. Her iconography and her symbolic representation resonate with me very deeply, especially as a Mother. The parasympathetic nervous system is a branch of the Autonomic Nervous System. The PNS is the calmative branch in direct relation to the activating sympathetic nervous system.

5: Resolute

1 - The Bhagavad Gita is a section of the Indian Epic Mahabharata. Read more:
https://en.wikipedia.org/wiki/Bhagavad_Gita
The version that I read each year is *The Bhagavad Gita in the Mahabharata* by J. A. B. Van Buitenen. Chicago: University of Chicago Press, 1981

2 - Thank you, Douglas and Appa, for sharing this beautiful line and teaching with students like me.

3 - Sourced from Judith H. Katz's handout, *Some Aspects, and Assumptions of White Culture in the United States.* Thank you, Myisha T. Hill and Constanza Eliana Chinea, for teaching me about these ideas.

4 - Kali is a powerful Hindu Goddess, more on her here: https://en.wikipedia.org/wiki/Kali

5 - See more about emergence in relation to pain in the book *Explain Pain: Supercharged by* G. Lorimer Moseley and David S. Butler, page 117-119.

6 - A few days before sending this to print a friend shared this quote. I do not know much about this author, but I am going to read up on him, because this quote is spot on. It speaks exactly to what I have been writing about. Disconnect in the Body and the visceral knowledge creates havoc. Here it is: "...Reich eventually came to realize that facism is not a peculiar characteristic of ephemeral political movements in Germany, Spain, Italy and Japan. It is a universal phenomenon precisely because it is rooted in the human body. When the multiple layers of bodily movements, impulses, and perceptions are not creatively transformed into creative movements in the direction of freedom, feelings for others, and purpose, people become easily subject to mass media and ideologies who foment populist movements fueled by fear and disorientation."
From Don Hanlon Johnson from *Diverse Bodies, Diverse Practices.*

7 - *Poised for Grace: Annotations on the Bhagavad Gita from a Tantric View* by Douglas Brooks.

8 - As of 9/29/2020, the United States death toll due to COVID-19 is estimated at 207,000 deaths. Information sourced from the *New York Times.*

9 - See chapter one in Douglas Brooks' *Poised for Grace* as listed above.

10 - Read about decision fatigue here: https://en.wikipedia.org/wiki/Decision_fatigue

11 - Dharma - This definition is from *Poised for Grace* by Douglas Brooks page 39. It is by far and away my favorite definition of the word and is at the base of my understanding. When I use this word. I think of this: *Dharma*: From the verbal root √*dhr*, which means "to make firm" and "to nurture and sustain," Dharma is filled with complementary and even contrary meanings. Its many nuances will be brought out in usage and context, but throughout the *Gita* it is the principle that establishes the foundation and support of all facets of reality. Dharma is not only a natural category but also a cultural and social one. It suggests the true potential of society to flourish through the establishment of justice, value, and prosperity. Dharma is principled argument, law, and the deep *feeling* that the world has spiritual value. Without Dharma we are doomed and with it we are held to rigorous accounts.

12 - I highly recommend this course by Constanza Eliana Chinea on Spiritual Bypassing:

https://emBodyinclusivity.teachable.com/p/unpacking-spiritual-bypass

13 - "The repair is in the wound." -Vishali

14 - For more books on self-regulation skills, I recommend:
- *Self-Reg* by Stuart Shanker. His website is - https://self-reg.ca.
- *The Body Keeps the Score: Brain, Mind, and Body in the Healing of Trauma* by Bessel van der Kolk.
- Follow @thrivinglittles on Instagram.
- *Hold On to Your Kids: Why Parents Need to Matter More Than Peers* by Gordon Neufeld and Gabor Maté MD

15 - Intersectionality is essential. The term was coined by black feminist scholar Kimberlé Williams Crenshaw in 1989. Check her out: https://aapf.org/podcast Read more here: https://en.wikipedia.org/wiki/Intersectionality
Then think about how this relates to you.

16 - Padashala has been a dream of mine for many years. With a group of powerful women's expertise, we have collaborated and created a neurocentric movement program for children and teens. I want to give credit and thanks to you all:
Alison C. Solomon
Amanda Faison
Jamie Donadio
Gina Stigi
Kelly Woodton
Krystal Kaiser
Diana Kwitnicki
Ellen Aumack

Julie Sobol
Melissa Ballone

17 - Abhinavagupta (c. 950 – 1016 CE) was a philosopher,
mystic, and aesthetician from Kashmir. Douglas Brooks
references him in *Poised for Grace*. Read more here:
https://en.wikipedia.org/wiki/Abhina.vagupta